St. Louis
BASEBALL HISTORY

St. Louis
BASEBALL HISTORY

· A GUIDE ·

BRIAN FLASPOHLER

FOREWORD BY JERRY REUSS, ST. LOUIS NATIVE & MLB PITCHER

THE
History
PRESS

Published by The History Press
Charleston, SC
www.historypress.com

Front cover, top left: Kathryn Flaspohler; *top center*: State Historical Society of Missouri; *top right*: Kathryn Flaspohler; *bottom*: Kathryn Flaspohler. *Back cover*: Kathryn Flaspohler.

First published 2022

Manufactured in the United States

ISBN 9781467151245

Library of Congress Control Number: 2022933363

CONTENTS

FOREWORD, BY JERRY REUSS   7

ACKNOWLEDGEMENTS   11

INTRODUCTION   13

CHAPTER 1: 1860–1899   17

*Baseball's Beginning in St. Louis…1861 Baseball Today…Time For Pro Baseball…
Battle Between the Colored Socks…Sportsman's Park…Leader of the Beer and Whiskey
League…Bellefontaine Cemetery…Calvary Cemetery…Lucas Wants a Team, Lucas
Starts a League…The Baseball Bible…Pitcher Throws BBs, Lays Bricks…Shocking
Accident…New Sportsman's Park*

CHAPTER 2: 1900–1926   49

*Brandishing a Mop Leads to Justifiable Homicide… Businessman Brings Browns
to St. Louis…Outlaws and Lefties… Lady Bee Inherits the Cardinals…Pugnacious
Patsy's Demise…Broeg Enters the World…Pitching Staff Wrecked…Don't Call
Him Jack…The Cardinals' Greatest Owner…Giants Played Here…The Birds on
the Bat Are Born…Doak Has an Idea…Gorgeous George Sizzles…A Mule, the
Devil and a Cool One…The Rajah at the Hotel Jefferson…Babe Ruth's Favorite
Brothel…Holy Cow, Carabina!*

CHAPTER 3: 1927–1947   89

*Baseball Lifer…Yogi….Not the Best Player on His Street…Muscles Does Not Walk
Like a Duck…Hall of Famer? Check the Night Shift…Fairgrounds Hotel…Rickey
Does Some Farming…The Whistle Blows, the Kid Rolls…The Cat Finds His*

Mouse…Heine Meine's Labor of Love…Hollocher's End…Roomies Southworth and Sewell…Is a Baseball's Terminal Velocity Fatal?…Girls Play Ball, Too…Beaumont High's Hall of Famer…Maya Angelou's Neighbor…The First Modern Sports Bar

CHAPTER 4: 1948–1974   125
Musial Becomes a St. Louisian…Major League High School…Stan Musial and Biggie's…Chase Park Plaza Hotel…Bow Wow Becomes an Undertaker…Anheuser-Busch Brewery…Youngster Witnesses Hero's Record…That Guy Really Delivers the Milk…The Redhead…Jack Buck Is Fired…Red Bird Bowling Lanes…Keane Quits…A Palace for Cardinals and Cardinals…Gibson Has a Year…An Artist on the Field and Off

CHAPTER 5: 1975–PRESENT   157
This Is Not Your Fantasy Football Plaque…The Moon Man Serves Meals… The Wizard's Sports Bar…The County Gets in on the Action…The Stars Shine Here…Mad Max…Cupples's Innovation…Jack's Final Rest…Sweet Lou Gives… Strawberry's Rehabilitation…The Final Gift…Lester's Sports Bar and Grill…Josh Hancock's Accident…Hall of Fame Philanthropist…The Voice of the Cardinals… Hall of Fame Cemetery…Uncle Charlie…Beep Ball…Busch Stadium…Soviet-Era Artist Carved "The Man"!?

CHAPTER 6: SUGGESTED TOUR ROUTES   199
The Major League Ballparks Tour… Hall of Famer Gravesite Tour…The Historic Buildings Tour

BIBLIOGRAPHY   209
INDEX   215
ABOUT THE AUTHOR   223

FOREWORD

*G*rowing up in my hometown of Overland, Missouri, in the 1950s and 1960s was quite a different experience than what it is today. Television was limited to stations covering the three major networks and a local independent station. Though a few FM radio stations dotted the landscape, AM radio was king. KMOX, the Cardinals' flagship station, wore the crown.

Before the advent of central air-conditioning, houses were cooled in the scorching St. Louis summers by window or ceiling fans with open screen doors and windows allowing the air to circulate. That led to a phenomenon of hearing the Cardinals broadcast emanating from each house in the neighborhood. When the Cardinals were on the air, it was conceivable to walk from one end of the block to the other and never miss a pitch!

But the Redbirds were not the only baseball game in town. My family lived just down the hill from what is now the Overland Post Office. Back then, it was the New Overland School. The baseball field was tucked neatly in a corner bordered by the dead end of Addie Avenue to the east, backyards of homes on Seneca Lane to the south and Woodson Road to the west. The field was the summer home of every kid who had a glove, bat or ball in the surrounding neighborhoods.

Usually, on a summer evening, one would find a team practice or a league makeup game in progress. My summer days were spent there through junior high as I secured my first employment as a summer counselor for the city in the early 1960s. The area where the field once stood is now a parking lot for the Overland Post Office.

Jerry Reuss (*second row, third from left*) with his fellow Khoury League All-Stars in 1960.
Jerry Reuss.

If games weren't available at New Overland, I joined another group of neighborhood kids on a well-kept lot between the Church of Nazarene and Ortmann Funeral Home located on Lackland Avenue just east of the Lackland/Woodson Road intersection. The playing surface was covered by grass and better suited for football games. We were asked not to play on Sundays during church services or when there was a funeral. Twenty or so years ago, I thought about those days, as both of my parents had their funerals at Ortmann. Today, a Walgreens drugstore sits on the southeast corner of the intersection and extends to the funeral home driveway—our memories paved over by a parking lot and shelves of hair care products.

Little League games were what really mattered. In the mid-1950s to the early 1960s, Legion Park, located at the corner of Midland Boulevard and Tennyson Avenue, was the first home of the ABC League. That is, until the population explosion of St. Louis County brought more kids who wanted to play into the Overland area than the field could handle.

Above: ABC Park field D today. *Kathryn Flaspohler*.

Left: Jerry Reuss's favorite photo of his playing days. *Los Angeles Dodgers and Jerry Reuss*.

Enter a few local real estate developers, who took an open space at 10050 Livingston Avenue in nearby St. Ann and converted the acreage into three baseball fields. I was joined by my brothers Jim and John, and ABC Park became a summer home for our family in the 1960s. With the three of us playing and both parents working, there were not many family dinners to share. There's no doubt in my mind that ABC Park played an integral part in shaping my major-league career.

Though the schoolyard and open field between the church and funeral home are long gone, ABC Park still stands. The fields are used year-round for baseball, softball, football and soccer. It is my sincere hope that ABC Park and fields like it scattered throughout the St. Louis area will produce other athletes that will live their major league dreams just as I did.

Inside this book, you will find stories about where players grew up, where they went to school, where they played, where they lived, where they worked, where they died and where they are buried. It is a great way to see St. Louis, through its rich baseball history.

—Jerry Reuss
August 24, 2021

ACKNOWLEDGEMENTS

I would never have been able to complete this book without a supportive team of people. I apologize, because I cannot list everyone, but these people deserve particular accolades. Fellow SABR member Carl Reichers, the world's best baseball fact checker, supplied the story about the Rawlings Gold Glove Awards and fact-checked the book. My brother Daniel for his copyediting skills, my brother Jason for reading early drafts and his brutally honest criticism and my sister Jennifer for bringing a sense of serenity to all family gatherings. SABR member and author Ed Wheatley gave great advice on marketing, copyright rules and more. Professor Greg Wolf helped focus the book and gave suggestions on how to approach publishers. All of the members of the St. Louis Bob Broeg SABR Chapter provided inspiration, especially Jeffrey Ecker for an early list of address ideas, Bob Giovanni for Kuebler Field information, Jim Leonard for Musial and Schoendienst home addresses, Steve Gietscher for *The Sporting News* addresses and information and Craig Carter for Bellefontaine information and his general interest in the project. Arkansas Robinson-Kell SABR member Fred Worth provided detailed gravesite information. Dan Arnold helped test out the suggested tour routes. Thanks also to The History Press's Chad Rhoad, who took a chance on a first-time author, and Rick Delaney and the production team, who did the hard work required to turn out the finished product.

A very special thanks to my lovely wife, Kathy, for her photography skills and her ability to put up with me, and to Dorothy and John for doing such a good job raising their favorite child.

INTRODUCTION

*I*n the days before cellphones and online tickets, most Cardinal fans have uttered the line, "Meet me at the Musial statue" when making plans to go to a game. The statue of Stan Musial is an iconic location in St. Louis baseball. This book explores this and many other locations where St. Louis baseball history took place.

It is a glimpse of St. Louis baseball history. It has to be a glimpse, because St. Louis has a long, rich baseball history. No city, aside from New York City, where the modern game started, has as much baseball history. This book covers people and events from the first documented baseball game under the "National Rules" in 1860 to the present day.

Each story cites a specific street address and highlights its relevance to baseball history. The addresses include major league ballparks, high school fields, players' homes and businesses, hotels and cemeteries. Other baseball-related addresses, such as *The Sporting News* and Rawlings Sporting Goods headquarters, KMOX radio, the trophy shop that supplied Rawlings' Gold Glove Awards, the church where the Cardinals iconic logo was invented and Babe Ruth's favorite home of ill-repute, are included. Each story touches on the history of the place or building.

Three suggested tours are included for the explorer who wants to see St. Louis through a baseball lens, some of which are well off the general tourist pathways.

Most people think the history of St. Louis major league teams is simple. The average fan believes the Cardinals have been around since the beginning of time and that there was a team called the Browns, which left for Baltimore a long time ago. The truth is more complicated.

Five major league franchises have called St. Louis home, along with three Negro League teams, now considered major league by Major League Baseball. Two teams were in the National Association, the first fully professional league, but not considered a major league by Major League Baseball. At various times, team names changed and some teams transitioned between leagues, but continuity of ownership and/or players is used to determine when a team is considered part of the same franchise.

For simplicity, I refer to the name that is relevant to the time period of the particular story and to the National Association as a major league. The accompanying table is a handy reference of all the St. Louis major league teams.

Franchise	Name	Years	League
St. Louis Brown Stockings			
	Brown Stockings	1875	National Association
	Brown Stockings	1876–77	National League
St. Louis Red Stockings			
	Red Stockings	1875	National Association
St. Louis Cardinals			
	Brown Stockings	1882	American Association
	Browns	1883–91	American Association
	Browns	1892–98	National League
	Perfectos	1899	National League
	Cardinals	1900–Present	National League

FRANCHISE	NAME	YEARS	LEAGUE
St. Louis Maroons			
	Maroons	1884	Union Association
	Maroons	1885–86	National League
St. Louis Browns			
	Browns	1902–53	American League
St. Louis Terriers			
	Terriers	1914–15	Federal League
St. Louis Stars (I)			
	Giants	1920–21	Negro National League
	Stars	1922–31	Negro National League
St. Louis Stars (II)			
	Stars	1937	Negro American League
St. Louis Stars (III)			
	Stars	1939–41	Negro American League

For the interested reader who wants to do further research, I highly recommend digging into the sources cited in the bibliography. In particular, the Society of American Baseball Research (SABR) Biographical Project is amazing. The audacious goal of this effort is to complete a four-thousand-word biography on every person who has ever put on a major league uniform. It is an ongoing effort, and so far over five thousand biographies have been completed. I use this resource extensively. Another critical source is Baseball Reference. This online database replaces the pre–internet age baseball encyclopedias and is an incredibly useful engine to provide statistics for today's baseball researcher.

Finally, I am always interested in feedback on this book and new addresses for my database. Please email me at brianflash100@gmail.com. I will read every note I receive. Additionally, I can provide customized guide services. Drop me a line if you are interested.

1

1860–1899

BASEBALL'S BEGINNING IN ST. LOUIS

Grand Boulevard and Natural Bridge Avenue (Northwest Corner)

Abner Doubleday did not invent baseball in Cooperstown, New York. The game evolved from bat-and-ball games played by children, of which the "New York Game" eventually dominated. The actual story of the start of baseball is complicated, but a group of gentlemen in New York City codified a set of rules in 1845. These men formed a club, the New York Knickerbockers, and played the New York Nine under these rules on the Elysian Fields in Hoboken, New Jersey, on June 19, 1846.

The game proved popular, but it took time to propagate. In 1857, the first convention of clubs was held and a new set of rules distributed. Other variants of baseball such as the "Massachusetts Game" and the "Philadelphia Game" died out. Brooklynite Merritt Griswold, who learned to play the New York game, moved to St. Louis in 1859. He organized the Cyclone Club in St. Louis, and others followed his lead. The *Missouri Democrat* printed the National Baseball Rules late in 1859. By 1860, there were four clubs in St. Louis learning the New York game.

The *Missouri Democrat* reported that the Cyclones and the Morning Stars met in Fairgrounds Park on July 9, 1860. This is the first documented baseball game played in St. Louis under the National Rules. The Morning Stars emerged victorious, 49–29. The game was played in a field west of the

Top: Fairgrounds Park in 1874. The game in 1860 was played to the west (*left*) of the round stadium. *Missouri Historical Society.*

Bottom: The Bear Pit façade in the southeast corner of the park. *Kathryn Flaspohler.*

main amphitheater, approximately across the street from the future location of Beaumont High School.

Fairgrounds Park started as a privately owned facility in 1856. It was the site of the annual St. Louis Exposition, an agricultural fair, from 1856 to 1902. The facility had two horse tracks and many other facilities for agricultural displays. A zoo (eventually absorbed by the St. Louis Zoo) was added in 1876. In 1903, the St. Louis Exposition was not held due to preparations for the 1904 World's Fair. The facility did not revive the exposition after the World's Fair and closed, hastened by Missouri's ban on horse-race gambling in 1905.

In 1908, the City of St. Louis bought the park and removed all the old buildings except for the bear pit façade, which survives at the southeast corner of the park. The neighborhoods around the park were the homes of generations of immigrants who played baseball. Professional baseball was played nearby in Sportsman's Park; this area was the epicenter of amateur baseball in St. Louis. When the St. Louis Cardinals moved downtown and with major demographic changes to the neighborhoods around the park, baseball in the area has mostly disappeared. The fields in the park have been converted to football fields for a new generation of St. Louis children. There are only hints of the old baseball fields, such as distance marker signs on fences.

1861 BASEBALL TODAY

Park Avenue and Missouri Avenue (Southeast Corner)

Lafayette Park is St. Louis's oldest public park. The thirty-acre park was set aside in an 1836 ordinance to prevent development and dedicated as a city park in 1851. Surrounding the park is the Lafayette Square neighborhood, a historic area filled with well-preserved homes. The statue of Thomas Hart Benton in the park dates to 1868, and the cast-iron fence around the park was installed in 1869. The park sits on a height above the neighborhood. When one looks at the meticulously maintained period homes surrounding the park, it is easy to imagine being here in 1861.

On March 6, 1861, four local baseball clubs, the Cyclones, Morning Stars, Empire and Commercials, met to play for the first time that year. The grounds were rough, causing players to trip and fall when fielding their positions. But the *Daily Missouri Republican* expected this to be remedied soon, as the Cyclones had petitioned the St. Louis City Council for permission to smooth the grounds at their own expense. That summer featured games between the clubs and other matchups, such as when club members divided according to marital status. One such match on July 4, 1861, resulted in the married men dispatching the bachelors, 55–32.

Lafayette Park was used for amateur ball for a few more years, but the heart of St. Louis baseball was farther north, and the park was improved for

Lafayette Park in 1875 is seen in this composite of four Compton and Dry map pages. No evidence of a baseball field existed then. *Library of Congress.*

St. Louis Perfecto Matt Moushey prepares to strike at a toss from a St. Louis Brown Stocking hurler. *Kathryn Flaspohler.*

An impending play at home. *Kathryn Flaspohler.*

other activities. In 2002, baseball returned. The St. Louis Perfectos, a team playing by the rules of the 1860s, was formed and selected the park as its home field. Other local teams followed, and now the St. Louis area is home to a half dozen or so vintage clubs.

A lucky summer weekend visitor may find costumed enthusiasts playing ball on the field in the northwest corner of the park. Pitchers will be tossing the ball underhanded. No one will be wearing gloves. The bats will be wood. With the historic neighborhood surrounding the area, it feels like a trip back in time. To guarantee a glimpse, search online for "St. Louis Perfectos vintage baseball" to find their schedule. For a special treat, attend the Shepard Barclay Festival the first weekend in June. This features teams from around the Midwest playing games all weekend.

TIME FOR PRO BASEBALL

1111 North Grand Boulevard

In 1867, Union Club president Asa Smith decided the best way to improve St. Louis's baseball reputation was to develop a great team. In order to have a great team, he needed the best players. Some type of incentive was needed to recruit the best players to his team.

The Union Club put a fence up around a field west of Grand Boulevard. The fence allowed the club to control access and charge admission to its games. The admission fees were used to maintain the grounds and to compensate players.

Thus the contest ended, the score standing at th-
close 113 for the Nationals, and 13 for the Union
Club.

It was evident from the start that the Union
boys were somewhat nervous and did not play as
well as usual, although the Nationals feely con-
ceeded that they displayed unusual skill and
energy.

We now present the score of the game:

SCORE.

Nationals.	H.	L.	R.	Unions.	H.	L.	R.
Parker, C. F		3	14	Meacham, 2d B		4	2
Williams, P		1	14	Freeman, C		3	4
Wright, 2d B		3	11	Cabanne		3	3
Fox, 3d B		3	14	R. Duncan, S. S		1	4
Studley, R. F		2	14	Prouty, 1st B		3	2
Fletcher, 1st B		3	12	Greenleaf, P		4	2
Smith, S. S		2	14	McCorkell, R. F		3	2
Berthrong, C		4	10	W. Duncan, C. F		3	3
Robinson, L. F		6	10	Asa Smith, L. F		3	3
Totals		27	113	Totals		27	26

INNINGS.

	1	2	3	4	5	6	7	8	9	
Union	2	4	0	9	1	0	1	1	8	— 26
National	0	28	4	25	8	11	18	13	6	— 113

Umpire—C. E. Coons, of the Empire Club, Washington.

Scorers—Messrs. Munson and Smith.

The club played the first game at the enclosed grounds on May 22, 1867.
It was an intrasquad exhibition game designed to show off the new park
features. On the east side of the grounds, near the Grand Boulevard entrance,
the club built a section of covered seats so ladies and their escorts had a good
viewing location protected from St. Louis's summer sun. On the south side
of the grounds, open bleachers were available for those hardy patrons who
could handle the heat. Home plate was located near the intersection of these
two sections of seating and faced northeast.

On July 22, 1867, the first game between a St. Louis team and a big
eastern team was held on these grounds. The National Base Ball Club of
Washington, D.C., was touring the country and came to St. Louis to meet
the Union Club. On a hot day, the Washington team sizzled, defeating the
Unions, 113–26. While the Unions were not yet good enough to compete

Opposite: The box score from the Washington victory. Only two items were noted: "HL" for hands lost (outs made) and "R" for runs scored. Daily Missouri Republican, *July 23, 1867*.

Right: St. Alphonsus Liguori Catholic Church today. *Kathryn Flaspohler*.

Below: The approximate location of Union Grounds home plate. *Kathryn Flaspohler*.

with the elite eastern teams, St. Louis proved a good place for the business of baseball, as about five thousand fans paid to attend the match.

Across the street, construction of the St. Alphonsus Liguori "Rock" Catholic Church began on May 1, 1867, less than a month before the exhibition game, with the cornerstone set on November 3. The church was dedicated five years later. The church is an impressive building, still in use today. In 2007, a lightning strike caused the roof and much of the interior to burn, but it has been rebuilt, and the congregation is still active. Immediately across the street is a vacant lot near where the Union Grounds home plate was located. The rest of the park is now occupied by businesses and homes.

Battle Between the Colored Socks

701 Compton Avenue

Only fourteen professional games were played at Red Stockings Park, but it is an important location in St. Louis baseball history. This is the southernmost in the string of parks that stretched through midtown and hosted all St. Louis professional teams until Busch Memorial Stadium opened in 1966. This key spot hosted the first professional league game in St. Louis in 1875.

The National Association, the first fully professional baseball league, formed in 1871. St. Louis did not have a team in the association until two teams signed up in 1875. St. Louis's first two entries into the National Association had very different beginnings. The St. Louis Brown Stockings were formed because local boosters were tired of amateur St. Louis teams being beaten by the professional Chicago White Stockings, the forerunner of the Chicago Cubs. In 1874, the White Stockings won all fourteen games played against the best St. Louis amateur teams by the combined score of 272–67. J.B.C. Lucas II, a wealthy real estate developer, was named president of the Brown Stockings and led the fundraising effort. Campbell Orrick Bishop, a wealthy St. Louis businessman and baseball aficionado, took the $20,000 raised and recruited players from Brooklyn and Philadelphia to play for St. Louis.

Local interests were disappointed that no St. Louis players were included on the Brown Stockings. They organized the best St. Louis amateurs and formed the St. Louis Red Stockings. Their cash resources were far less than the Brown Stockings, but they hoped local ties would entice large crowds.

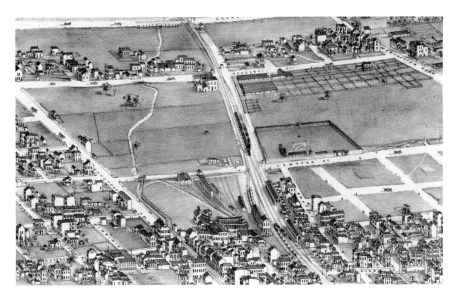

Compton and Dry map view of Red Stockings Park in 1875 (*no. 4, right of the railroad tracks*). *Library of Congress.*

They enclosed the existing park on Compton Avenue for their home field and built bleachers for one thousand people. Home plate was located just south of where Compton Avenue crosses the current railroad tracks and faced northwest toward center field.

On May 4, 1875, the Brown Stockings met the Red Stockings for the first professional league game in St. Louis. One of the Brown Stocking shareholders appraised the teams in an interview years later: "Every one of the Brown Stockings was of massive mold and great experience while the Reds were mere striplings with limited experience." Great weather drew a capacity crowd eager to see the first St. Louis professional teams. No one expected the Reds to win. The main betting action involved whether the Red Stockings would score more than five runs.

The Brown Stockings scored two in the second and single runs in the third and fourth, then eight runs in the sixth due to the Reds' poor fielding. No players wore gloves, so errors were much more common then. The Reds were shut out until scoring a single tally in the sixth. The fans betting on the over five runs must have been discouraged. The Browns scored twice in the seventh to stretch the lead to 14–1. However, in the bottom of the eighth, the Reds staged a comeback, scoring eight runs on "some of the best batting ever seen in St. Louis." The Brown Stockings eventually stopped the rally and tallied a single run in the ninth to finalize the score at 15–9.

View of the Metro facility looking southeast toward the park location. *Brian Flaspohler.*

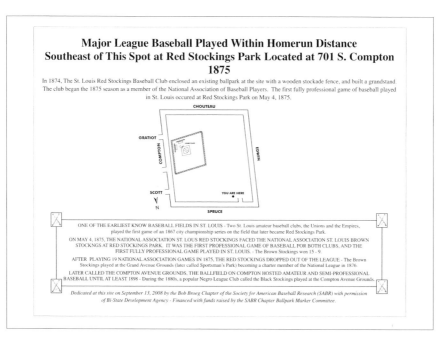

Major League Baseball Played Within Homerun Distance
Southeast of This Spot at Red Stockings Park Located at 701 S. Compton
1875

In 1874, The St. Louis Red Stockings Baseball Club enclosed an existing ballpark at the site with a wooden stockade fence, and built a grandstand. The club began the 1875 season as a member of the National Association of Baseball Players. The first fully professional game of baseball played in St. Louis occured at Red Stockings Park on May 4, 1875.

ONE OF THE EARLIEST KNOW BASEBALL FIELDS IN ST. LOUIS - Two St. Louis amateur baseball clubs, the Unions and the Empires, played the first game of an 1867 city championship series on the field that later became Red Stockings Park.

ON MAY 4, 1875, THE NATIONAL ASSOCIATION ST. LOUS RED STOCKINGS FACED THE NATIONAL ASSOCIATION ST. LOUIS BROWN STOCKNGS AT RED STOCKINGS PARK. IT WAS THE FIRST PROFESSIONAL GAME OF BASEBALL FOR BOTH CLUBS, AND THE FIRST FULLY PROFESSIONAL GAME PLAYED IN ST. LOUIS. - The Brown Stockings won 15 - 9.

AFTER PLAYING 19 NATIONAL ASSOCIATION GAMES IN 1875, THE RED STOCKINGS DROPPED OUT OF THE LEAGUE - The Brown Stockings played at the Grand Avenue Grounds (later called Sportsman's Park) becoming a charter member of the National League in 1876.

LATER CALLED THE COMPTON AVENUE GROUNDS, THE BALLFIELD ON COMPTON HOSTED AMATEUR AND SEMI-PROFESSIONAL BASEBALL UNTIL AT LEAST 1898 - During the 1880s, a popular Negro League Club called the Black Stockings played at the Compton Avenue Grounds.

Dedicated at this site on September 13, 2008 by the Bob Broeg Chapter of the Society for American Baseball Research (SABR) with permission of Bi-State Development Agency - Financed with funds raised by the SABR Chapter Ballpark Marker Committee.

Detail of the on-site historical marker. *Bob Broeg Chapter of the Society for American Baseball Research.*

Unfortunately, the Red Stockings were not able to draw enough interest to stay in the league. They played nineteen games, going 4-15, before being dismissed from the league for failure to make a road trip. The more competitive Brown Stockings won the city's heart and finished the season in fourth place in the National Association, including an emphatic postseason series victory over the Chicago White Stockings for the unofficial "Championship of the West." The Compton Avenue Grounds remained a ball field for amateur teams but was eventually redeveloped. Currently, the MetroBus Central Facility occupies the site along with railroad tracks. A historical marker identifying the ballpark is located at the entrance of the MetroBus facility just off Spruce Street.

SPORTSMAN'S PARK

Dodier Avenue and Grand Boulevard (Northwest Corner)

Sportsman's Park is baseball hallowed ground. For years, it was the site where the most major league baseball games were played. In recent times, it has been overtaken by Wrigley Field and Fenway Park, but the next active site on the list, Dodger Stadium, will require another forty seasons before it surpasses Sportsman's Park for the number of major league games played at a single location.

Professional league baseball started here in 1875, when the original St. Louis Brown Stockings entered the National Association. This first professional league folded after the season, replaced by the new National League. The Brown Stockings transferred to the National League and played the 1876 and 1877 seasons until financial woes and a gambling scandal caused their demise. The park had a simple wood grandstand with capacity for about three thousand, and home plate sat in the southeast corner of the site.

The next team to call Sportsman's Park home was the new St. Louis Brown Stockings, which played in the American Association in 1882. Chris von der Ahe renovated the park, moving home plate to the northeast corner of the site and increasing capacity, first to six thousand and then twelve thousand. Von der Ahe converted a home in right field to a beer garden. For the first few years, the beer garden was in play. A spectator enjoying one of von der Ahe's cellar-chilled brews could find themselves bowled over by an outfielder chasing a long fly ball!

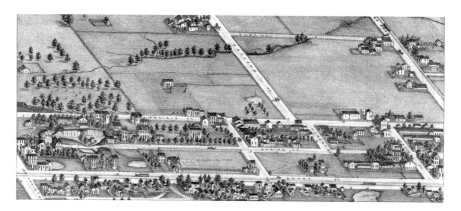

Sportsman's Park on the 1875 Compton and Dry map. *Library of Congress.*

Little remembered today, the Browns won four consecutive American Association pennants at the park. In 1886, they played a World Series against the National League's Chicago Cubs (then called the White Stockings). After three games in Chicago, the teams moved to St. Louis to decide the outcome. St. Louis won the first two games in Sportsman's Park, taking a 3-2 lead in the series. Chicago led 3–0 in game six until St. Louis rallied for three runs in the bottom of the eighth. After a scoreless ninth and top of the tenth, outfielder Curt Welch scored on a wild pitch in the bottom of the tenth, winning the game and the series for St. Louis. His scoring play entered baseball lore as the "$15,000 slide," named for the speculated amount of money awarded to the winning team.

Von der Ahe's Browns vacated the park in 1893 to play in new Sportsman's Park on Natural Bridge Avenue. Therefore, it was available when the American League St. Louis Browns moved to the city from Milwaukee in 1902. The wood grandstands were rebuilt, and park capacity was increased to 15,000. Home plate was repositioned to the northwest. A major rebuild in 1908 reoriented home plate to the southwest corner of the site, where it would remain. Grandstands were rebuilt, increasing capacity to 34,000. The St. Louis Cardinals moved to the park in 1920 as the Browns' tenants. For the next thirty-three years, both teams called Sportsman's Park home, and every major league team played here. The Browns left for Baltimore after the 1953 season, leaving the stadium to the Cardinals, who continued playing here until the downtown Busch Memorial Stadium was ready in 1966.

Sportsman's Park hosted four premodern World Series (1885–88), including the disputed tie series in 1885 and the Browns' victory over Chicago in 1886. In the modern era, ten World Series were held here, with

Left: A classic view of the park in its final configuration. *Missouri Historical Society*.

Below: The view toward center field today. The historic YMCA building is prominent. *Kathryn Flaspohler*.

the Cardinals winning seven. In 1944, the Browns and Cardinals met in the World Series, and Sportsman's Park hosted all the games. This has only happened four times in baseball history, and once since the St. Louis series, in the COVID-shortened year of 2020.

When the Cardinals moved to Busch Memorial Stadium, the site was donated to the Boys & Girls Clubs of St. Louis. The organization maintains a facility there today as a safe place for neighborhood youth to participate in sports. The field now is occupied primarily by a football field and tennis courts. A large billboard on the outside of the Boys & Girls Club building highlights Sportsman's Park facts.

Leader of the Beer and Whiskey League

2801 North Grand Boulevard

At the close of the 1880 season, August Solari, who owned the lease on Sportsman's Park, decided he would not renew it. Chris von der Ahe, a German immigrant who ran a grocery and saloon on Grand Avenue, took over the lease. He knew nothing about baseball but appreciated the large crowds that frequented his establishment when there were baseball games.

Chris von der Ahe in 1886. *Missouri Historical Society.*

Von der Ahe, on advice from his bartender and former major leaguer Ned Cuthbert, renovated the field and grandstands to allow more spectators. After a successful 1881 amateur season, von der Ahe, representing St. Louis, joined five other owners and formed the American Association for the 1882 season.

The American Association successfully competed against the National League as a second major league. It drew more fans by having lower ticket prices (twenty-five cents instead of fifty cents), Sunday games and alcohol sales in the parks. This positioned the league to appeal to the working class, and newspapers soon called it the "Beer and Whiskey League." Von der Ahe was a major driving force in these innovations.

The St. Louis Browns stayed in the AA for all ten years of the league's existence. They won four consecutive pennants from 1885 to 1888 and one World Series, defeating their rival, the Chicago White Stockings, in 1886. Von der Ahe made a fortune on his popular baseball team, using baseball to help market his saloon business, which grew to a half-dozen locations in the city.

Von der Ahe's fortunes declined in the 1890s. The extravagant and womanizing owner divorced his first wife and, failing to learn from that experience, divorced his second. He built a new park for the St. Louis Browns, but two stadium fires, including a serious one in 1898, completed the evaporation of his fortune. His team was sold at auction before the 1899 season in order to pay his creditors.

Von der Ahe was reduced to tending bar to make ends meet. He also received money from his former team captain, Charles Comiskey. He died

Right: The Golden Lion Saloon before its demolition in the 1930s. *Missouri Historical Society*.

Below: Modern view of the Golden Lion Saloon's location. *Kathryn Flaspohler.*

of cirrhosis in 1913 and is buried in Bellefontaine Cemetery. His team continues to this day, now called the St. Louis Cardinals, and his legacy of alcohol sales in the stands and promotional gimmicks to draw fans is continued by every baseball team.

The home and grocery store is long gone, having been demolished in the 1930s. The site was occupied by Carter Carburetor from 1920 to 1984, during which time it was contaminated by PCBs and put on the EPA Superfund list for cleanup. It is now being remediated. A golf facility for inner-city youth is planned.

Bellefontaine Cemetery

4947 West Florissant Avenue

Early in 1849, a group of prominent St. Louis businessmen organized the purchase of a farm north of St. Louis for a new cemetery. It was pressed into service quickly, as a major cholera epidemic struck the city in 1849, killing over four thousand people, about 10 percent of the population. Medical thought at the time blamed "bad air," and cemeteries were considered a significant source. A number of city cemeteries were exhumed and the occupants re-interred in the new Bellefontaine Cemetery. As an added bonus, this removal cleared space for new development in the city core.

Bellefontaine is a nondenominational cemetery and the final resting place for over 87,000 people. Senator Thomas Hart Benton, explorer William Clark and Anheuser-Busch cofounder Adolphus Busch rest here, to name a few. Impressive monuments are abundant, including the Louis Sullivan–designed Wainwright Tomb, which is in the National Register of Historic Places.

Many significant baseball figures are interred here, including *The Sporting News* executives J.G. Taylor and Charles Spink, St. Louis Browns owner

Wainwright Tomb. *Kathryn Flaspohler.*

Chris von der Ahe's impressive monument. *Kathryn Flaspohler*.

Philip Ball and Campbell Orrick Bishop, one of the leaders who organized St. Louis's first professional baseball team. Frank Bradsby, of famed bat maker Hillerich and Bradsby, is also here, along with a handful of former major league players. The most prominent of the baseball figures is Chris von der Ahe, the man who founded the St. Louis Cardinals.

Von der Ahe has an impressive monument despite his dying penniless. When he was leading the successful St. Louis Browns and wealthy from his saloon and grocery business, he commissioned a large statue of himself. After his passing, the statue was repurposed into his monument and remains today. His grave is located in Block 162, lot 2953 at GPS coordinates N 38° 41.396', W 90° 13.733'.

Today, Bellefontaine Cemetery occupies 314 acres, one-third of which is unused. It is a wonderful place to wander to view the historical monuments and take in the excellent views overlooking the Mississippi River. It is popular with bird-watchers due to its location on many bird migratory routes, ensuring that many different species are seen. History buffs appreciate the excellent historical tours the cemetery offers about the people buried here.

CALVARY CEMETERY

5239 West Florissant Avenue

Calvary Cemetery is a Roman Catholic cemetery founded in 1854, in part due to the cholera epidemic that struck St. Louis in 1849. Catholic cemeteries in the town center were filled after that disaster, and more space was needed. At first, the new cemetery was outside the city limits, but as St. Louis grew, development surrounded the 470-acre burial ground. Prominent figures buried here include General William Tecumseh Sherman, Dred Scott, Tennessee Williams and one of the founders of St. Louis, Auguste Chouteau.

Calvary Cemetery contains three hundred thousand people and is the final resting place of eighty-six major league players along with three baseball executives and three umpires. More major league ballplayers are buried here than in any other cemetery.

Urban Shocker, the possessor of one of the best names in baseball history, played seven seasons for the St. Louis Browns and won 20 or more games four years in a row. He is the best pitcher in Browns franchise history, winning 126 games for the team. He played for the Yankees before

Above: Urban Shocker family monument. *Kathryn Flaspohler*.

Right: George "Jumbo" McGinnis's weathered headstone. *Kathryn Flaspohler*.

Joe Blong in the Dowling family plot. *Kathryn Flaspohler.*

and after the Browns but maintained his home in St. Louis. He died twelve days before his thirty-eighth birthday from a combination of pneumonia and heart disease. He is buried in Section 24, lot 3313 (N 38° 42.313', W 90° 14.566').

George Washington "Jumbo" McGinnis started and won the first game in St. Louis Cardinals franchise history. He was the ace of the St. Louis Browns from its beginnings as an amateur team in 1879 and continued as it became a major league team in 1882. McGinnis won 77 games over the first three seasons of the team's history and picked up 11 more wins in a supporting role, until he was traded in 1886. He worked as a glass blower before and after his major league career and remained in St. Louis until his death in 1934. He is buried with his wife in Section 25, lot 377 (N 38° 42.145', W 90° 14.560').

Joe Blong is one of five St. Louis natives who made their professional debuts on May 4, 1875, for the National Association St. Louis Red Stockings. These five share the distinction of being the first major league players born in St. Louis. Blong had the longest career of the five, playing three seasons for St. Louis, batting a scrawny .216. The University of Notre Dame alumnus died on his thirty-ninth birthday, in 1892. He is buried in Section 12, lot 290 (N 38° 41.875', W 90° 14.118').

The cemetery is still active today. According to the Archdiocese of St. Louis, at current interment rates, there is room for at least three hundred more years of burials. The location, like Bellefontaine Cemetery, overlooks the Mississippi River and is an interesting place to take in the wonderful historic monuments.

LUCAS WANTS A TEAM, LUCAS STARTS A LEAGUE

Jefferson Avenue and Cass Avenue (Northeast Corner)

Henry Lucas lived and loved baseball. His older brother J.B.C. Lucas helped fund the first professional St. Louis team, the original St. Louis Brown Stockings. Henry wanted his own team in his hometown. The National Agreement, baseball's governing body, gave the current St. Louis Browns of the American Association full territorial rights to the city, which prevented Lucas from starting a St. Louis team in the National League.

Lucas would not be denied. With his inheritance, he started his own major league, the Union Association. He recruited owners in seven cities to start

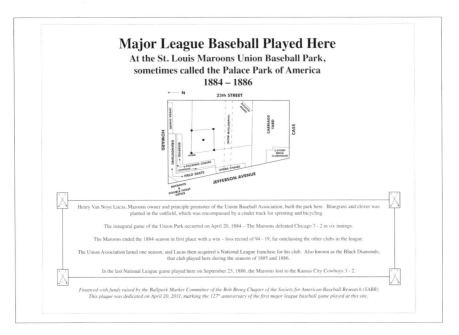

Line drawing layout of the Union Association Park. *Bob Broeg Chapter of the Society for American Baseball Research.*

their own teams, and they played a season in 1884. Due to their red uniform trim, his team was known as the St. Louis Maroons.

Lucas's team needed a stadium, so he built the Union Association Park. The primary entrance, which included the ticket office and grandstand, was located at the southeast corner of Jefferson Avenue and Howard Street. The wood grandstands held ten thousand patrons at full capacity. Home plate faced center field toward Twenty-Fifth Street and Cass Avenue. The three-story player clubhouse was on the northeast corner of Jefferson and Cass, beyond right field. Lucas spent over $15,000 for his park and included a cinder track around the field to accommodate running and cycling events. It was Lucas's "Baseball Palace," and he planned to use it for many years.

Lucas also used some of his inheritance to attract quality players from the existing major leagues. No other owner in the Union Association spent so lavishly. The Maroons were the class of the league, going 94-19, 21 games ahead of the Cincinnati Outlaw Reds. No other St. Louis baseball team has ever had a higher winning percentage.

It turned out that the Maroon dominance was terrible for the league. Attendance dropped rapidly when no cities had a pennant race to follow. The more established National League and American Association had the

Artist rendition of the new National Geospatial-Intelligence Agency headquarters campus.
National Geospatial Intelligence Agency.

capital to survive the war, but the Union Association owners had no stomach for it. The league folded, and Lucas was allowed to move his Maroons into the National League. They were much less successful against the stiffer competition, finishing last in the eight-team league in 1885 and sixth in 1886 before Lucas sold the team to Indianapolis interests. Lucas's "palace" was used by amateur teams for two more years then was torn down in 1888.

There were several commercial buildings on the site over the years. Brown Shoe Company maintained a warehouse and offices here for a time. Today, the new headquarters of the National Geospatial-Intelligence Agency, currently under construction, covers the site.

THE BASEBALL BIBLE

Tenth Street and Olive Street (Southwest Corner)

The Sporting News was founded by newspaperman Alfred H. Spink. Spink was active with the American Association St. Louis Browns but had the entrepreneurial spirit needed to start a national newspaper. The first issue was published on March 17, 1886. Soon, the paper became one of the most popular sports weeklies in the country, competing with *Sporting Life*, published in Philadelphia. The first issue was published from a building at 11 North Eighth Street, a site now occupied by St. Louis City Garden.

Alfred's younger brother Charles bought in to the business and by the late 1890s owned the paper outright.

As circulation grew, the headquarters moved to various buildings in downtown St. Louis. The office found a more permanent home in the Pennsylvania Building at Tenth and Olive in 1910. Charles died in 1914, and his son John George Taylor Spink took over the paper. He was the single most important driving force behind the business. His tireless work ethic, large file of personal contacts and willingness to call anyone at any time set the example for his employees. He also ruled the office "with an iron will and an iron fist." As baseball became the most popular sport, *The Sporting News* devoted more and more of its space to the sport. In 1924, *Sporting Life* ceased publication; *The Sporting News* was the "Baseball Bible," a title it would retain for the rest of the century. The paper stayed in the Pennsylvania Building for thirty-six years, its longest tenure at any address, before moving to a building on Washington Avenue.

Spink's long leadership of the paper led to his status as a leading icon in baseball reporting. After he died in 1962, the Baseball Writers' Association of America instituted the J.G. Taylor Spink Award, the highest award given to its members.

The four-story Pennsylvania Building, designed by H.F. Roach, was constructed in 1908. It replaced buildings that had provided homes for the city's immigrant Irish population, including brothers Jack and Bill Gleason, the first third baseman and shortstop, respectively, for the St. Louis Cardinals franchise. They lived in a tenement building here in 1880.

The Pennsylvania Building's upper three floors were converted to lofts in 2003. The ground floor is now occupied by Jack Patrick's Bar and Grill,

The Pennsylvania Building in the early 1940s. *Missouri Historical Society*.

The Pennsylvania Building today. *Kathryn Flaspohler.*

a quirky downtown dive bar with favorable reviews and a loyal clientele. Large crowds frequent the bar before and after Cardinal games and other downtown events.

As the media landscape changed, *The Sporting News* relocated to Charlotte, North Carolina, in 2007. The paper ceased print publication 5 years later after a 126-year run. In 2020, Lindenwood University in St. Charles acquired *The Sporting News* archives and is cataloging the collection to make it available to researchers.

PITCHER THROWS BBS, LAYS BRICKS

2907 Magnolia Avenue

Few today remember Charles "Silver" King, so nicknamed for his head of white hair. The last time he pitched in a major league game was over 125 years ago, and he is not in the Hall of Fame. However, the St. Louis native was an outstanding pitcher.

King, son of German immigrants, grew up in a house located where the Anheuser-Busch Brewery complex sits today. He was a side-arming twenty-

Right: Silver King's 1888 Old Judge Cigarette card. *Library of Congress*.

Below: Silver King's home on Magnolia (*left*), next to similar homes. *Kathryn Flaspohler*.

year-old who threw with great pace when he delivered a pitching season that boggles a modern observer's mind. Pitching for the 1888 St. Louis Browns, he started 64 games. A modern pitcher will start fewer than half that number. He completed all 64 starts! The last time a league saw that many was the 66 hurled in the American League in 2015. But that was the total for all the pitchers in the entire league. King even pitched in relief twice. He threw a total of 584 2/3 innings. In 2019, five starters in the National League pitched more than 200 innings; the leader threw 209. King did the work of more than two and a half modern starters in a 137-game season.

The Browns won their fourth consecutive pennant with a record of 92-43, King notching victories in 45 of those wins. His 1.63 ERA led the league. The team lost its postseason series against the National League New York Giants, 6 games to 4, King going 1-3 in his five postseason starts. The season, measured by the new sabermetric statistic Wins Above Replacement, rates as the tenth-most valuable single-season pitching performance of all time.

Baseball was a very different game then. It is a tough argument to claim that King had the tenth-greatest pitching season of all time, due to the differences in how pitchers are used today. But he had a great season and was a great pitcher. He won 112 games in three excellent seasons for the St. Louis Browns and 91 more in seven years for other teams.

After his career, the sturdy gentleman with massive hands returned to St. Louis and followed in his father's footsteps, becoming a bricklayer and contractor. King was prosperous, moving his family to the large house on Magnolia sometime before 1900. He paid off the mortgage by 1910 and remained there until his death in 1938. He is buried in his family plot in New St. Marcus Cemetery at 7901 Gravois Road. His home, built in 1889, is a sturdy, single-family residence in the Tower Grove East neighborhood and retains the character of the historic neighborhood.

SHOCKING ACCIDENT

2400 North Twenty-Second Street

Sons of Irish immigrants, brothers Jack and Bill Gleason were teammates on the St. Louis Browns. Jack was the third baseman and Bill the shortstop starting with the amateur team's organization in 1879. In 1882, the Browns became a charter member of the new American Association, a major league to rival the National League.

The 1883 St. Louis Browns, including Jack Gleason (*sixth from left*) and Bill Gleason (*second from left*). *Alfred H. Spink.*

"Handsome" Jack Gleason was a favorite of the ladies, but after the 1882 season, the Browns wanted to improve at third base and signed Arlie Latham for 1883. A disgruntled Jack played some outfield, then was sent to Louisville for the rest of the season. He came back to St. Louis to play for the Maroons of the new Union Association in 1884. For most of 1885, he was banned by Major League Baseball for his participation in the outlaw Union Association. The ban was lifted, and in 1886, he played for Philadelphia. He retired after the season.

In 1881, Jack and Bill both worked for the St. Louis Fire Department. While their jobs may have been secured by Browns owner Chris von der Ahe, it was not a job for show. Both men were real firefighters, fulfilling all the duties of the job. Jack was injured fighting a fire before the 1881 season. Newspapers speculated that he might not be able to play, but he recovered before the season.

By 1893, Jack was a member of Engine No. 5 and worked out of the firehouse on 2400 North Twenty-Second Street. On June 22, 1893, he leaned out of the second-story window of the firehouse and contacted a live wire attached to the station's arc lights. He received a severe shock to his right side and was confined to bed for over a month. The *St. Louis Post-Dispatch* story reported, "Had the floor been wet Gleason would have been instantly killed."

Gleason recovered, but firefighting was dangerous. Injured fighting a blaze in 1901, he was unable to return to full duty. The department assigned him as a fire watchman. Those duties included monitoring the fire tickers

Firehouse No. 5 early in the twentieth century. *Robert Pauley, curator, St. Louis Fire Department Museum.*

and dispatching help as required. He died at the age of ninety in 1944, his disabilities apparently not impacting his longevity.

The Engine No. 5 firehouse was taken out of service in 1953 after seventy-seven years of use. It remained a warehouse before it was torn down in the 1970s. Today, the lot is part of the new National Geospatial-Intelligence Agency campus, which started construction in 2019 and is scheduled to be completed by 2025.

NEW SPORTSMAN'S PARK

3836 Natural Bridge Avenue

In 1892, the owners of the largest streetcar company in St. Louis planned a new line to pass next to Fairgrounds Park. At the same time, Browns owner

Chris von der Ahe wanted a new ballpark for his St. Louis Browns. These interests collided, and von der Ahe inked a fifteen-year lease for a two-block area bounded by Natural Bridge Avenue, Vandeventer Avenue, Ashland Avenue and East Prairie Avenue.

St. Louis architecture firm Beinke and Wees designed a grand, new wood ballpark for the location. Due to the lopsided size of the plot of land, the dimensions of the field were asymmetrical. Home plate and the primary grandstand sat nearest to the intersection of Vandeventer and Natural Bridge. Left field was an enormous 470 feet from home plate. Center field stretched as far away as 500 feet, while right field was a cozy 290 feet from the plate. Von der Ahe included a horse-racing track around the field and a "Chute the Chutes" thrill ride that operated during the game. Boatloads of eight passengers would careen down a water-filled incline in an early version of a modern-day log ride.

The new ballpark was referred to in the papers as "New Sportsman's Park" and was praised. The *St. Louis Post-Dispatch* wrote, "[The park] certainly ranks as one of the best conceived, prettiest, and thoroughly practical arrangements in any park in the country." The paper also proudly mentioned the conveniently arranged set of ladies' toilet rooms in back of the grandstand.

The park suffered issues over the years. There were severe fires in 1898 and 1901. Lawsuits resulting from the 1898 fire cost von der Ahe his fortune and his baseball team. An operator of the thrill ride was killed in 1896 during a doubleheader between the Browns and the Louisville Colonels. He jumped into the water to rescue a passenger's hat. The next boat came down the chute and crushed him. The baseball games continued as scheduled.

Artist rendition of Robison Field in an 1893 newspaper ad. *Missouri Historical Society.*

Robison Field location today; the outfield was where the football field is today. *Kathryn Flaspohler.*

Despite these tragedies, the park served as home field for the St. Louis Cardinals for twenty-seven years. After the Robison brothers bought the team in 1899, the park became known as Robison Field. By 1920, it was the last wood park in the major leagues, and it suffered from serious structural issues. Cardinal management Sam Breadon and Branch Rickey made a deal to become tenants of the American League St. Louis Browns and sold the park to the St. Louis Public School District, using the proceeds to pay off the team debts and invest in Rickey's new minor league farm system.

The school district built Beaumont High School on the site, opening the school in 1926. Beaumont was closed in 2014, but the magnificent high school building is still partially occupied today.

1900–1926

Brandishing a Mop Leads to Justifiable Homicide

6116 Dr. Martin Luther King Boulevard

Pat Hynes was born in 1884 to Irish immigrants living in North St. Louis. He was a phenom, playing for the amateur Ben Miller team at age thirteen and advancing to the semipro St. Louis Trolley League by his late teens. At nineteen, he played his first professional season, in 1903, for the Vicksburg Hill Billies, a Class D minor league team. He split time as a pitcher and an outfielder, putting up a 7-4 record pitching and batting .257. At the end of the 1903 season, the last-place St. Louis Cardinals (45-93 record) gave the southpaw a one-game tryout. The team lost his start to the Philadelphia Phillies, 6–3, and he went 0-3 at the plate.

Hynes started the 1904 season on baseball's banned list due to contract jumping from Vicksburg. He returned to the Trolley League and played well. In early August, the St. Louis Browns engineered a deal to make him eligible and added him to their roster. He played the outfield, batting .236 for his half season and pitched a handful of times, the highlight being a complete-game win against the Detroit Tigers.

In 1905 and 1906, Hynes returned to the minors, playing for Minneapolis and Milwaukee, sometimes sparring with management. He threatened to quit and go back to his bartending job in St. Louis unless his salary was increased. Milwaukee, happy with his play, signed him for the 1907 season.

BASEBALL PLAYER KILLED
IN QUARREL OVER TWO BEERS

PATRICK J. HYNES.

Right: Pat Hynes from the *St. Louis Post-Dispatch* in 1907. St. Louis Post-Dispatch.

Below: Easton Road, looking east from the city limit in the 1920s. The café occupies the storefront where Harry Grover's saloon was. *Missouri Historical Society*.

On the evening of March 11, with his bags packed for spring training with Milwaukee, Hynes went out with a friend. The pair visited several drinking establishments before going to Harry Grover's saloon on Easton Road in the early-morning hours of March 12. The two each had a beer and asked the bartender for a second. The bartender asked them to pay for the first two. Hynes refused, telling the bartender they were on the house.

The argument escalated. Hynes threw an empty pretzel bowl and then a spice holder. The missiles proving ineffective, he grabbed a mop and headed toward the barkeep. When he went behind the bar, the threatened taverner pulled a revolver and fired two shots. One missed, but the other inflicted a fatal wound. A grand jury dismissed the charge against the bartender, finding in favor of his self-defense claim. Hynes is buried in Calvary Cemetery in St. Louis.

Easton Road was renamed Dr. Martin Luther King Boulevard in 1972. Harry Grover's saloon is long gone. The site was occupied by a convenience store, which burned down in 2020. The lot is now vacant.

Businessman Brings Browns to St. Louis

5700 Cates Avenue

Robert Hedges was born near Kansas City in 1869. His father died when he was ten, and his brothers were killed in the infamous 1886 Kansas City tornado. He overcame these obstacles and made his fortune in the buggy business, selling out when he foresaw the automobile was going to be a major disruptor to the buggy industry.

Hedges was not a sportsman. Purely as a business investment, he bought a minority share of the American League Milwaukee Brewers. The team's weak finances during its sole year in Milwaukee reduced the team's value. Hedges saw the opportunity and bought shares. He moved the team to St. Louis, then the fourth-most populous city in the country, for the 1902 season.

Hedges rebranded the team the St. Louis Browns, taking the name from the American Association team that won four consecutive pennants in the 1880s. The vacant Sportsman's Park became his team's home.

Due to player discontent with Cardinal management, Hedges was able to lure many Cardinal players to his Browns. The team was very competitive, finishing second in the American League and outdrawing the Cardinals by 46,000 fans on the season. The high finish would not be repeated until 1908,

Above: Robert Hedges in 1911. *Library of Congress.*

Left: The Hedges home on Cates Avenue today. *Kathryn Flaspohler.*

when his veteran pitchers pushed the team to a fourth-place finish, only six and a half games behind the pennant winner. The personable "Colonel Bob" made a big profit on the season and undertook a massive renovation to Sportsman's Park, building a new concrete-and-steel grandstand and moving home plate to its final location at the northwest corner of the block.

The Browns were a second-division team every season except 1902 and 1908. The impatient Hedges was tired of losing and began looking for a buyer. The Federal League war gave him his opportunity. When the Federal League folded in 1915, St. Louis Terriers owner Philip Ball bought the Browns from Hedges for $450,000, nine times what Hedges paid ten years earlier.

When Hedges owned the Browns, he lived at 5700 Cates Avenue. The home, located in the West End neighborhood, was built for him in 1905. The neighborhood's proximity to Forest Park made it a jewel to live in, and mansions are located throughout. After World War II, the area deteriorated as population left the city and the demographics of the area shifted. Hedges's home had become dilapidated by the late 2000s but was purchased in 2019. The new owner performed an extensive renovation, bringing the home back to life. The gray-brick structure is a testament to restoring historic homes instead of demolishing them.

OUTLAWS AND LEFTIES

Grand Boulevard and Laclede Avenue (Southeast Corner)

The years 1914–15 was a heady time for St. Louis baseball fans. Three major league teams were in town. The American League St. Louis Browns played in Sportsman's Park, the National League St. Louis Cardinals held court at Robison Field and the Federal League St. Louis Terriers were in Handlan's Park.

The Federal League began as an outlaw minor league in 1913. It didn't follow Major League Baseball's national set of rules, and this enabled it to steal players away from those teams, thus the "outlaw league" moniker. Emboldened by a successful 1913 season, the Federal League declared itself a major league for the 1914 season.

Alexander Handlan, a railroad supply entrepreneur, owned land at Grand and Laclede. The Terriers' owner, refrigerator magnet Philip Ball, leased the property and built a wood ballpark with the main grandstand at

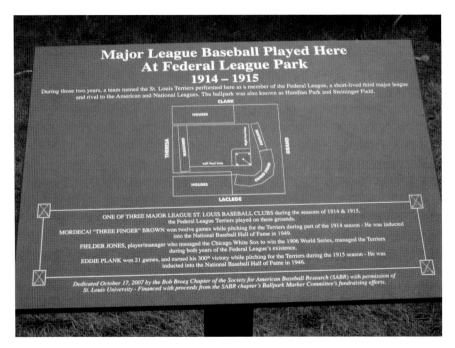

The marker, now missing, denoting Handlan's Park. *Bob Broeg Chapter of the Society for American Baseball Research.*

the corner of Laclede and Grand. Home plate sat here facing the southeast. More seating ran parallel to Laclede, down the left-field line, ending at third base. The park held fifteen thousand fans.

Ball's Terriers were terrible in 1914, finishing last in the league. A much-improved team in 1915 finished 87-67, second place by mere percentage points behind the 86-66 Chicago Whales. Southpaw Eddie Plank had an excellent year. He won 21 games, including the September 11 home game against the Newark Peppers. This was his 300th career win, the first time a left-handed pitcher reached this total in major league history.

The Federal League folded after the 1915 season, but Handlan's Park was still used for baseball. On October 5, 1916, St. Louis baseball fans saw one of the great unknown pitchers of the early twentieth century.

Left-handed John Donaldson used a lively fastball and a big curve to carve up batters for thirty seasons. He was born in Glasgow, Missouri, in 1891 and was pitching professionally by 1911. When his career ended in 1940, he had won over 400 games as a left-handed pitcher while striking out more than 5,000 batters. Why isn't more known about him? Because he was barred from the major leagues for being Black.

Left: John Donaldson. *Society for American Baseball Research.*

Right: The West Marchetti Tower. *Kathryn Flaspohler.*

For most of Donaldson's career, he barnstormed throughout the United States and played games against teams in every town imaginable. He played several times in St. Louis, but the October contest marked the only documented time he pitched in the city. His All-Nations took on the Negro St. Louis Giants in a tightly contested game. Donaldson fanned eight Giants, and his All-Nations held a 2–1 lead into the ninth inning. In the ninth, a Donaldson wild pitch allowed the tying run to score, and the game ended in a 2–2 tie.

The park was used by St. Louis University until the wood stands were condemned in 1928. For many years, the land was used for circuses, carnivals other events. The Grand Tower Apartments were built on site in the early 1960s. Now owned by St. Louis University, the apartments, now named the Marchetti Towers after Father Jerome Marchetti, provide on-campus housing for sophomore and junior students.

Lady Bee Inherits the Cardinals

4215 Lindell Boulevard

Helene Hathaway Britton was daughter and niece, respectively, of St. Louis Cardinals owners Frank and Stanley Robison. She was born in Cleveland in 1879. The young lady was well educated, but her family encouraged her interest in baseball, the family business. She married Schuyler Britton in 1901 and had two children. Her father, Frank, died in 1908, and her uncle Stanley passed away in 1911. Stanley's will deeded controlling interest of the team to her. This made the thirty-two-year-old the first female owner of a major league baseball team.

The other National League owners were aghast at a woman in their midst. The male-dominated media and the other owners expected Britton to sell the team. She refused. They tried to bar her from owner meetings, but she insisted they allow her in. She was active in league business discussions and in running her team. She locked horns with Cardinal manager Roger Bresnahan after the 1912 campaign. She fired him after he exclaimed, "No woman can tell me how to run a ball game!" The media dubbed her "Lady Bee" and granted her grudging respect in print.

In 1913, in response to a rule change among the owners, Britton purchased a home in St. Louis on Lindell Boulevard and made Schuyler the team president. However, she remained the power behind the throne. The Cardinals were not a good team, but Britton did what she could to draw fans. She started a Ladies' Day promotion—escorted women were admitted free—and hired a singer to perform between innings.

Helene Britton with other National League owners in 1912. *Library of Congress.*

Britton's mansion site (*right*), next to a period home converted to a law office. *Kathryn Flaspohler*.

Schuyler, a cruel man and an alcoholic, was not a good partner. They reconciled several times, but she divorced him in 1917. Her fortune was tied up in the Cardinals, and she lacked money to upgrade the deteriorating ballpark, so she sold the team to businessman Sam Breadon for $350,000 in 1918 and returned to Cleveland.

She remarried and moved to Philadelphia, where both her children and her four grandchildren lived. She passed away in 1950.

The Britton home on Lindell no longer exists. The American Cancer Society's Hope Lodge, a place for cancer patients and their families to stay while receiving treatment, occupies the site. A home immediately to the west, now used as a law office, is from the period and gives the visitor a glimpse into what Lindell looked like when Lady Bee lived there.

Pugnacious Patsy's Demise

410 Locust Street

Oliver "Patsy" Tebeau grew up in the Irish neighborhoods in old North St. Louis in the late 1860s and early 1870s. His father was French Canadian, and his mother was German, but Tebeau took the mannerisms, accent and nickname from the Irish people he grew up with.

Patsy was a combative leader during his major league career. He was an average player, but his leadership was recognized early, and he became a player-manager by the time he was twenty-five years old. He led the National League Cleveland Spiders for most of the 1890s, finishing second in the league three times and winning the postseason series for the Temple Cup once. This was a violent period in baseball history, and Tebeau was no exception. During a brawl in the mid-1890s, he was upset that his star pitcher, Cy Young, did not join in the fray. He expressed his displeasure, calling out Young and noting that everyone on the team would play and fight together. Brawls and rowdy incidents over the years drove the National League to institute rules in 1898 to curb the cursing and rowdiness rampant in baseball.

Patsy Tebeau on an Old Judge cigarette card. *Goodwin and Company*.

Tebeau moved to the St. Louis Cardinals in 1899, along with a large portion of the Cleveland team. Frank and Stanley Robison owned both teams and sent the best players to St. Louis, as attendance was better there than in Cleveland. The depleted Spiders had the worst season in baseball history in 1899 and folded. Tebeau managed St. Louis through 1900, retiring to focus on his saloon business.

Tebeau's saloon, the Court Bar, was profitable. Reports noted that he was a perfect gentleman and friendly to all those he had tangled with during his baseball days. As the years passed, his health declined and his personal life suffered. In 1917, his wife left him, returning to Cleveland. In early 1918, he made a trip to French Lick, Indiana, to use the hot springs to cure his rheumatism. Unfortunately, he did not get any relief and was just as ill when he returned.

On the morning of May 16, 1918, his bartender found Tebeau's body in the back office of the saloon. He had taken his own life with a revolver. The gun was tied to his hand, apparently to ensure that his death would not be mistaken for a homicide. A note on his desk requested that the authorities notify his wife and his brother, former major league player George.

The Security Building, circa 1920. *Missouri Historical Society*.

The Court Bar was located in the Security Building. This historic structure was designed by Peabody, Stearns, & Furber and built in 1892 in what was then the city's financial district. The stately, eleven-story granite-and-brick building is listed in the National Register of Historic Places and is one of the last remaining tall office buildings from that era in St. Louis.

The Security Building today. *Kathryn Flaspohler.*

It has undergone significant restoration over the years and is still used for offices. The interior lobby is an attractive space, but the exact location of the Court Bar is lost. One tenant, the Bellefontaine Cemetery Association, has continuously rented office space in the building since it was erected.

Broeg Enters the World

4628 Virginia Avenue

Bob Broeg (rhymes with "egg") was a titan of St. Louis sports, starting at the *St. Louis Post-Dispatch* in 1946 as its baseball writer. He covered the local teams and wrote five weekly columns on all sports, but he particularly loved his Cardinals and the Missouri Tigers football team. He never retired, penning his last column in 2004, one year before his death. He was a prolific author, writing or contributing to over twenty books. He hosted, with his friendly rival Bob Burnes, a radio show on KMOX for many years. He received a multitude of awards, including the J.G. Taylor Spink Award.

Broeg was born in the kitchen of the duplex at 4628 Virginia Avenue. His birth was not without trouble. As Broeg wrote, "So in the afternoon in the kitchen at Virginia and Pulaski in South St. Louis, Madame Mal Practice used her forceps like ice tongs, grabbing me fore and aft, rather than left and right. One tong scarred my left eye, permanently blurring my vision. No corneal transplants back then. The other tong dug into the back of my cranium. So, yeah, I had a hole in my head from day one." His father chased the midwife off and fetched a doctor to the house to patch the infant up.

Bob Broeg Chapter SABR logo. *Bob Broeg Chapter of the Society for American Baseball Research.*

Bob Broeg's childhood home today. *Kathryn Flaspohler.*

Broeg was a lifelong St. Louis resident. He learned his writing at Mt. Pleasant Grade School and honed his style at Cleveland High School and at the University of Missouri in Columbia, majoring in journalism. After serving in the United States Marines Corps during World War II, he took a job in Boston but returned to St. Louis soon after. The St. Louis Chapter of the Society for American Baseball Research is named in honor of Bob Broeg, and he attended chapter meetings for many years, sharing his insights to the delight of the other members.

Broeg had his own inimitable style. A classic sentence lifted from a Stan Musial column he wrote showcases his comma-heavy and sometimes meandering style, "In his greatest season, 1948, when he batted a savage .376, leading the league in everything except taking tickets, The Man was a .361 hitter over the same number of games played by the Cardinals this year and had knocked in 18 runs with an extra base display that included four doubles, four triples and four homers."

The red-brick duplex at Virginia and Pulaski in the Dutchtown neighborhood was built in 1908, ten years before young Broeg came along, and it remains a family residence today.

PITCHING STAFF WRECKED

956 Hamilton Avenue

During the spring of 1919, St. Louis wanted to get back to a sense of normalcy. World War I had ended the previous November, and the Spanish flu pandemic had waned. The St. Louis Cardinals, coming off a dreadful quarter century in which they never finished higher than third and finished last seven times, did not have high expectations but needed to get back to work. Due to postwar travel restrictions and to save money, the team remained in St. Louis for spring training, staying at the luxurious Hamilton Hotel.

On the morning of April 16, starting pitcher Lee Meadows drove to the park in his new Chevrolet. Pitchers Willie Sherdel, Oscar Horstman, Bill Doak and Leon Ames were passengers. At Union Boulevard and Ashland Avenue, Meadows collided with a streetcar. All five pitchers suffered injuries, including Meadows, who was thrown through the front windshield. The immediate reporting at the time was understandably concerned. A team

The Hamilton Hotel in the 1920s. *Missouri Historical Society.*

Left: Lee Meadows with the Pirates. In 1915, he became the first spectacled player since 1886. *Pittsburgh Pirates*.

Below: The Hamilton Hotel today. *Kathryn Flaspohler*.

only carried eight or nine pitchers, and to lose five at once was a catastrophe. The seriousness of the injuries was unknown. Within two days, reporting noted that the injuries were not too serious. The accident was attributed to Meadows failing to brake on time in the wet conditions.

All five pitchers were able to start the season for St. Louis. Unfortunately, the team was dreadful in 1919, finishing seventh. Horstman pitched very little, marking the end of his major league career. The other four pitched all season at varying levels of effectiveness. Doak, Meadows and Sherdel all went on to have long major league careers. The best of the trio, "Wee" Willie Sherdel, still holds the Cardinal franchise record for wins by a left-handed pitcher (153).

The Hamilton Hotel was built in 1903, designed by St. Louis architecture firm Barnett, Haynes and Barnett. The Beaux-Arts building was constructed to fill anticipated demand with the upcoming 1904 St. Louis World's Fair. The structure, four stories tall plus a basement, was eight blocks from Forest Park and about three miles from Robison Field, the Cardinals' home field. Advertisements from the time speak of the building's excellent amenities, including "rapid elevator service, safe deposit vaults, many books in the hotel library, special parlors and dressing rooms for ladies, private telephones, a roof garden, bowling alleys, billiard rooms, a children's playground, and Turkish baths."

The Hamilton Hotel underwent extensive interior renovations in 1954 for conversion to a convalescent home. It was closed in the early 1970s but received new life in the 1980s, when it was converted to an apartment building, which it still is today. The exterior of the building, with minor exceptions, retains its historic appearance and is a grand edifice in the neighborhood.

Don't Call Him Jack

3848 Shenandoah Avenue

Three people named John Tobin have played in the major leagues. Oddly, none of the three is referred to by his given name in baseball records. St. Louis native John Tobin, when an active player, was referred to by teammates and local media as "John" or "Johnny." But oddly, he still ended up in the record books as Jack.

Tobin was born in St. Louis in 1892. He grew up on LaSalle Street, a bricklayer's son. His schooling ended after grade school, and he worked for the electric company as a lineman. But his heart was in baseball. He played on several amateur teams and was signed by the Texas League Houston Buffaloes but never reported, likely figuring the money as a lineman was better. When the hometown St. Louis Terriers of the new Federal League came calling, he signed.

The Federal League was an independent minor league in 1913. Tobin played well for the Terriers in his first professional experience. The following year, the league declared itself a major league, and the Terriers kept Tobin in their outfield. He was a solid performer as the youngest regular on the team, hitting .270 and fielding reliably in right. In 1915,

Left: Johnny Tobin in 1922. *Library of Congress.*

Right: Tobin's home on Shenandoah. *Kathryn Flaspohler.*

both Tobin and the Terriers were much improved. He hit .294 and led the league in at bats and hits.

The Federal League folded after the 1915 season, and Tobin was picked up by the St. Louis Browns. After a year of minor league seasoning, he came back to St. Louis and held an outfield spot for eight seasons. From 1920 to 1924, he and fellow Brownie outfielders Bill "Baby Doll" Jacobson and Ken Williams hit over .300 each season with one exception: Tobin hit .299 in 1924, one hit away from what would have been an amazing five-year statistical run.

During his stretch of excellence, Tobin lived on Shenandoah Avenue with his wife and daughter. His Shaw neighborhood home, just north of Tower Grove Park, was built in 1899. It has been converted into a two-unit building but remains a private residence. Tobin, after his baseball career, coached, worked for the fire department and sold cars. He enjoyed hunting and fishing in his spare time. He died in 1969 and is interred in Calvary Cemetery in St. Louis.

THE CARDINALS' GREATEST OWNER

4701 Westminster Place

Sam Breadon. *Missouri Historical Society.*

The St. Louis Cardinals have had a number of excellent owners in their long history. The founder of the team, Chris von der Ahe, presided over four consecutive pennants and navigated the team's move to the National League when the American Association folded. Beer baron August Busch II was a strong community supporter who provided needed capital to keep the team in St. Louis and drove construction of a new downtown stadium. Current owner Bill DeWitt II has led the team through a quarter century of consistent competitiveness and was the driving force behind the current stadium. Sam Breadon, however, stands above these men.

Breadon, born in New York in 1876, arrived in St. Louis to join two friends in an automobile concern. The ambitious Breadon wanted to own his own garage, so the other two men fired the upstart. In order to survive, he won the popcorn concession for the St. Louis World's Fair. With profits from that venture, he bought his own garage. His honesty and work ethic impressed an executive in the Western Automobile Company, who hired him. In a few short years, he worked his way up to president and owner of the business. The company owned the exclusive rights to sell Pierce-Arrow automobiles.

By 1915, Breadon, a baseball fan, had bought stock in the St. Louis Cardinals. When Helene Hathaway Britton sold her shares in 1918, he led the investment group that purchased them. He became president and continued to buy shares until he had majority control.

During this period, he and his wife, Rachel, and their adopted daughter lived on Westminster Place. The three-story home, a mix of Tudor and Arts and Crafts styles, was built in 1909. It was located a block from the headquarters of the Western Automobile Company and a mile from Sportsman's Park.

Breadon, with Branch Rickey as his operational mastermind, turned the Cardinals from a perennial cellar dweller into a consistent winner and world champion. During his twenty-seven years as owner, the Cardinals won

Breadon's home on Westminster today. *Brian Flaspohler.*

nine pennants and six world championships. In the late 1930s, he sold the automobile business to focus on the Cardinals.

In 1947, Breadon, feeling his age, sold his share of the Cardinals to put his estate in order. He received $3 million (about $36 million today), an excellent return on his initial investment in the team. He died in 1949 at the age of seventy-three from liver cancer. He was cremated, and his ashes were scattered over the Mississippi River by airplane near Chester, Illinois. The home on Westminster, built in 1909, remains a single-family residence today.

GIANTS PLAYED HERE

North Broadway and East Clarence Avenue (Southeast Corner)

The St. Louis Giants was an African American amateur baseball team that played in St. Louis from at least 1906, run and organized by Charles Mills. In 1919, Mills built a new grandstand at an existing park owned by the Kuebler family. The *St. Louis Argus* wrote of the construction: "The new stands at the

Historic photo of a game at Giants' Park. *Norma Kuebler Taaffee.*

park will be finished by this Saturday. They are being built of entirely new, dressed lumber and will accommodate more than 5,000 persons."

When Rube Foster started the Negro National League in 1920, Mills's Giants was an inaugural team. Mills expanded the grandstands, adding 100 more feet of stands along Clarence and 90 more feet along Broadway. He added a bleacher section in center field. Home plate sat nearest to the Clarence and Broadway intersection, facing southeast. Left field, bounded by Prescott Avenue, was somewhere ɔund 360 to 400 feet, while Holly Avenue kept the right-field distance closer to 300 feet, favoring left-handed hitters.

In 1921, Mills got the best left-handed hitter he could find, future Hall of Fame center fielder Oscar "The Black Ty Cobb" Charleston. Charleston responded in a huge way. He hit .433 with 15 home runs and 91 RBIs, leading the league in all three categories. Behind Charleston, who was also frequently compared to Babe Ruth in the newspapers, and left-handed-hitting right fielder Charlie Blackwell (who hit .405), St. Louis improved from sixth in 1920 to third in 1921.

Right: Oscar Charleston, whom Bill James ranked as the fourth-best ballplayer ever. *National Baseball Hall of Fame and Museum*.

Below: Current view of the Giants Park site. *Brian Flaspohler*.

After the 1921 season, Mills was forced to sell the team to new interests in St. Louis. The new owners changed the team name to the Stars and built a new stadium, Stars Park, closer to the African American neighborhoods of St. Louis. Charleston moved on to the Indianapolis ABCs and continued his amazing play for many more seasons.

Giants Park remained a baseball facility and was used as late as 1937, when the St. Louis Stars of the Negro American League played a few of its home games there. By 1950, the park was gone, replaced by the McCabe and Powers Auto Body Company. Today, the site is an abandoned concrete parking lot, overgrown with brush, leaving no evidence of the Giants who played here.

THE BIRDS ON THE BAT ARE BORN

Clay Street and Church Street (East of Clay)

Before 1900, the St. Louis Cardinals were called the St. Louis Browns, named for the brown trim on their uniforms. In 1900, the team changed the trim to red. The story goes that a female fan saw the uniform and said, "My, that's a lovely shade of cardinal." A passing sportswriter heard the remark, and the new name was born. The name had nothing to do with the scarlet bird so common in the eastern United States, and the uniforms had no birds on them.

Cardinal catcher Gus Mancuso sporting an early birds-on-the-bat uniform. *Missouri Historical Society*.

On February 16, 1921, Branch Rickey was scheduled to speak to the Men's Fellowship Club at the First Presbyterian Church in Ferguson, Missouri. With an important guest expected, Allie Mae Schmidt wanted some nice decorations for the meeting. She planned a red carnation bouquet for each table's centerpiece but was looking for an extra touch.

While considering the problem, she saw two cardinal birds visible against the white snow outside of the window. Inspiration! She made a template of a cardinal, cut the shapes out and hand-colored each decoration. She roosted each bird on a brown string representing a tree branch.

First Presbyterian Church at the end of Church Street. *Ferguson Historical Society*.

Rickey loved it. Schmidt's father, Edward, was seated at the same table as Rickey, and they discussed the birds as a symbol for the team. Edward ran the art department of a printing company and provided samples to Rickey several days later. One sketch showed a single bird on a bat; another concept showed two birds balanced on a bat.

A year later, the Cardinals' uniforms featured two birds on a bat. While the logo has been tweaked many times, the concept is the same as in 1922: two birds balancing a bat on the uniform front. For Allie Mae's contribution to the best logo in sports, the Cardinals awarded her a lifetime pass to their baseball games in 1937.

Looking east on Church Street today. *Brian Flaspohler.*

The First Presbyterian Church moved to 401 Darst Road in the late 1920s. Church Street ended at Clay Street in 1921. The original location of the church is covered by Church Road, now extended to Elizabeth Avenue. A private home on the northeast corner of the intersection is the closest building to the original location.

Doak Has an Idea

2317 Lucas Avenue

In 1887, brothers George and Alfred Rawlings opened a sporting goods store on the northeast corner of Eighth and Chestnut Streets in downtown St. Louis. They sold sports equipment, including guns and fishing supplies. An office building now occupies the site.

In 1898, the duo, financed by Charles Scudder, began manufacturing sports equipment. They made baseballs, gloves, football pads, uniforms and other items. They won the contract to supply uniforms to the St. Louis Cardinals in 1906, leading to a long relationship with professional baseball.

Until 1920, ball gloves from Rawlings and all other manufacturers had each finger separated. Veteran Cardinal pitcher Bill Doak, known as "Spitting Bill" for his then legal use of the spitball, had an idea. He attached

Left: Rawlings newspaper ad featuring a Bill Doak glove. St. Louis Globe-Democrat.

Below: The Rawlings facility converted into a St. Louis public school. *Brian Flaspohler.*

the thumb and forefinger of a standard glove with leather, creating a pocket. He patented the idea and approached Rawlings. The company licensed the idea and marketed the Bill Doak model glove. Soon, the glove with a pocket became the industry standard. The pocket made it much easier to catch and hold on to a baseball and revolutionized defense. Rawlings, already a large supplier of gloves, became the primary supplier to professional players. The Doak model was available and sold for over thirty years, earning Rawlings and Doak a small fortune.

Rawlings occupied an office and manufacturing plant on Twenty-Third and Lucas from early in the twentieth century to 1950. Doak gloves were manufactured there along with other equipment. After Rawlings moved, the warehouse continued to be used by other interests. In the early 2000s, the warehouse was refurbished into a charter school. Today, a KIPP St. Louis public charter school occupies the Rawlings location where Bill Doak gloves were introduced.

Rawlings remains a St. Louis company. Its headquarters is in Town and Country, a St. Louis suburb. It is the sole supplier of balls to Major League Baseball and is a primary supplier of gloves to players. It continues to manufacture uniforms, protective gear and other items.

GORGEOUS GEORGE SIZZLES

2303 North Geyer Road

George Sisler is the greatest player in St. Louis Browns history. His hitting, fielding and high baseball IQ impressed everyone. He was inducted into baseball's Hall of Fame in 1939.

When he was seventeen years old, Sisler signed a contract with the Pittsburgh Pirates. St. Louis Browns executive Branch Rickey, who knew about Sisler from his time at the University of Michigan, informed the league that the youngster was under age, and the contract was invalidated. He then signed Sisler to a contract with the Browns. Sisler had no regrets and maintained a lifelong positive relationship with Rickey.

In 1915, Sisler's first year with the Browns, he pitched in 15 games and was effective. Rickey also used him at first base and in the outfield and was more impressed with Sisler as a position player. He hit .285 and fielded well. Rickey made him the full-time first baseman in 1916, and Sisler responded with a .305 batting average.

In 1917, Sisler started a six-year run during which he hit .377, including a gaudy .420 during the 1922 season. The Browns were not normally a competitive team, but 1922 was an exception. They were involved in a tight pennant race with the New York Yankees. Sisler hurt his shoulder near the end of the season but still played. During a late-season home series against the Yankees, a fan threw a bottle and hit Yankee center fielder Whitey Witt, knocking him out. The Browns, shaken by their fans' behavior, lost the game and ended the year one game behind New York. Despite the late-season injury, Sisler still led the league in batting average, runs scored, hits, triples and stolen bases and was named Most Valuable Player.

At the peak of his abilities, the twenty-nine-year-old suffered a case of the flu, which led to a terrible sinus infection. Doctors performed a nasal operation that affected his eye muscles, resulting in double vision. Sisler, talking of the issue later, said: "One day I was driving I thought I saw two cars in the other lane. There was only one, and I knew something was drastically wrong." His vision did improve through the summer but was not good enough to enable him to hit a baseball in competition. He missed the entire 1923 season.

From left: George Sisler, Babe Ruth and Ty Cobb. *Library of Congress.*

Sisler's marker on the columbarium. *Kathryn Flaspohler.*

The historic Old Meeting House Presbyterian Church. *Kathryn Flaspohler.*

Sisler's vision continued to improve, and he returned in 1924, but he was not the same. He had good seasons after his infection but not to his previous standards. However, he had a career .340 batting average and was a member of the fourth class inducted into the Baseball Hall of Fame.

After Sisler retired, he co-owned a sporting-goods store and started a softball league in St. Louis. He became involved with the National Baseball Congress. When Rickey went to Brooklyn, he hired Sisler as a scout and coach. Sisler followed Rickey to the Pittsburgh Pirates in the same roles but moved back to St. Louis in 1957. He and his wife, Kathleen, had three sons, two of whom, Dick and Dave, played in the major leagues. Sisler died in 1973 and is interred in the Old Meeting House Presbyterian Church Cemetery on Geyer Road. His grave (N38° 37.358', W90° 25.211') sits behind the historic stone church built by settlers to the area in 1834. In 2009, Seattle Mariners outfielder Ichiro Suzuki paid his respects to George Sisler five years after he broke Sisler's seventy-four-year-old record of most hits in a season. In 1978, the church was placed in the National Register of Historic Places and is used today for special services and events.

A Mule, the Devil and a Cool One

Compton Avenue and Market Street (Northeast Corner)

In 1922, in the heart of Mill Creek Valley, an African American community, St. Louis Stars owners Richard Kent and Sam Sheppard built a new stadium for their newly purchased team. It would mark the first time a Black team played in a stadium built specifically for their use. The Negro National League was the highest level Black players had the opportunity to compete at, being barred from the major leagues. The Stars' stadium was within walking distance and near a trolley stop, making it easy to reach for the African American fans of their local team.

The wood grandstands held ten thousand fans and were shaped to fit the site. Due to a street that no longer exists, the left-field fence was a cozy 250 feet from home plate. A large trolley car building was beyond the fence. A 35-foot wall, like Boston's Green Monster, was an attempt to keep things fair for pitchers. The outfield dimensions grew quickly as the fence reached center field, to at least 425 feet. James "Cool Papa" Bell's legendary speed was needed to cover that huge expanse of grass.

Left: The only known photo of Stars Park. *Missouri Historical Society.*

Below: The 1926 St. Louis Stars. George "Mule" Suttles and Willie "The Devil" Wells are the first two standing on the left. James "Cool Papa" Bell is sitting fourth from right. *National Baseball Hall of Fame and Museum.*

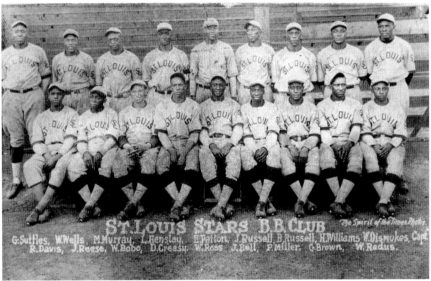

ST. LOUIS STARS B.B. CLUB *The Spirit of the Times Photo.*

G. Suttles, W. Wells, M. Murray, L. Hensley, E. Patton, J. Russell, B. Russell, H. Williams, W. Dismukes, Capt.
R. Davis, J. Reese, W. Bobo, D. Creasy, W. Ross, J. Bell, P. Miller, G. Brown, W. Redus.

The St. Louis Stars was a championship aggregation of players. The team showcased three future Hall of Famers on the field: the aforementioned Bell, Willie "The Devil" Wells at shortstop and George "Mule" Suttles in left field. This trio led the Stars to league pennants in 1928, 1930 and 1931. The team's winning percentage over those seasons was a hefty .718—183 wins verses 72 losses.

Due to the Great Depression and financial issues, the Negro National League folded after the 1931 season. The Stars' owners sold the land back to the city for $100,000.

The current Stars Park marker. *Kathryn Flaspohler.*

In the late 1950s, the entire Mill Creek Valley area was demolished in an ill-conceived and brutally executed urban renewal project. More than five thousand buildings were demolished, and a community of twenty thousand people was displaced. Public investment in the area did not materialize as expected, so St. Louis University and Harris Stowe State University bought large sections of land.

Through pure happenstance, Harris Stowe's baseball field sits on the ground once occupied by Stars Park. The diamond is oriented in the same direction, shifted slightly east. A historical marker, placed by the St. Louis Bob Broeg SABR Chapter, is located on the site. Harris Stowe has embraced the history, naming its field Stars Park.

THE RAJAH AT THE HOTEL JEFFERSON

415 North Tucker Boulevard

Rogers Hornsby is the greatest right-handed hitter in St. Louis Cardinals history and arguably one of the greatest of all time. He started with St. Louis as a nineteen-year-old in 1915, playing a handful of games at the end of

Rogers Hornsby doing what he did best. *Oklahoma Historical Society.*

the season. From 1916 to 1918, he was their full-time shortstop and a very productive hitter. He even led the league in triples and total bases in 1917.

At the end of the 1918 season, he married Sarah Martin. The marriage was doomed. Not only was Rogers a tough person to live with, but by 1923, he was seeing a married woman, Jeanette Pennington Hine. In 1923, he both completed a divorce with Sarah and settled a lawsuit filed against him by Jeanette's husband. Soon, Rogers and his paramour moved into the Hotel Jefferson.

The "Rajah's" personal life had no impact on his ability to hit. In 1923, during his off-field divorce and lawsuit troubles, he hit .384; in 1924, he bounced back to .424, an average not reached since by any player. In fact, from 1920 to 1925, he had a stretch of offensive dominance rivaled only by Babe Ruth and Barry Bonds. He led the National League in batting average, on-base percentage and slugging percentage each of those six seasons. He also won the batting Triple Crown in 1922 and the Most Valuable Player Award in 1925.

In 1926, as a player and manager, he led the St. Louis Cardinals to their first modern World Series win, over the favored New York Yankees. But it wasn't enough to keep him on the Redbirds. Cardinals owner Sam Breadon was quoted as saying, "Listening to Hornsby is like having the contents of a rock crusher dumped on one's head." Breadon traded Hornsby to the New York Giants after the 1926 season for Frankie Frisch, who, while not "The Rajah," did have an excellent career in St. Louis, leading the team to four World Series appearances, winning two of them.

Hornsby was an amazing hitter who had many personal faults. He was gruff and had no diplomatic skills whatsoever. Once, when sitting at a table with shortstop Eddie Farrell, a reporter asked Rogers about the team's chances of wining a pennant. He famously responded, "Not with Farrell playing shortstop." He also had a penchant for gambling on horses and never went to a movie because he thought it was bad on his eyes. While terrible with ownership and teammates, Hornsby was good with children. George Sisler also lived in the Hotel Jefferson, and Rogers would take Sisler's son and friends for a cola or ice cream.

After the trade, Hornsby became something of a journeyman, spending seasons in New York, Boston and Chicago before returning to St. Louis to play and manage, mostly unsuccessfully, for the Cardinals and the Browns.

The Hotel Jefferson was opened in 1904, anticipating visitors in St. Louis for the World's Fair. The Classical Revival building, designed by architecture firm Barnett, Haynes, and Barnett, was one of the most sought-after places to stay in St. Louis. It hosted many conventions and society events, including housing the delegates for the Democratic National Conventions in 1904 and 1916. By 1920, it was still being described by the *St. Louis Post-Dispatch* as "ranking with the most notable hostelries in the country. It is absolutely fireproof, of steel construction, and an artistic design." In 1928, a

Right: The Hotel Jefferson before the 1928 addition. *Missouri Historical Society*.

Below: The Hotel Jefferson today. *Kathryn Flaspohler*.

large addition was built, doubling the number of hotel rooms. After several ownership changes, the hotel closed in 1975. Two years later, it reopened as a senior living center. In 2006, the remaining seniors were relocated and plans were made to convert the building into condominiums, but financing collapsed. The vacant building, on the National Register of Historic Places, was purchased in 2018. New renovation plans are in place to convert the building for hotel, apartment and retail use.

Babe Ruth's Favorite Brothel

4021 Forest Park Avenue

Babe Ruth was a frequent visitor to St. Louis during his career, as the Boston Red Sox and New York Yankees played (and frequently beat) the lowly Browns. He enjoyed his visits to the city, because he could fatten his average on the Browns' subpar pitchers and because he enjoyed the women in local houses of ill repute. "St. Louis has the best prostitutes in the American League!" exclaimed the Babe. Maybe the old saying about the Browns—"First in shoes, first in booze, last in the American League"—should have included "first in babes."

Legendary sportswriter Bob Broeg reported in the *St. Louis Post-Dispatch* years later, "Babe Ruth, arriving by train from Chicago, would have sent his bag to the hotel—his roommate often saw only the Babe's suitcase for days—and he'd have hied himself to his favorite St. Louis brothel on Forest Park Boulevard for an evening of booze, broads, and black cigars."

Babe Ruth in 1922, uncharacteristically not surrounded by admirers. *Library of Congress.*

Building
contemporary with
May Traynor's
establishment at 4007
Forest Park Avenue.
Brian Flaspohler.

May Traynor ran the Babe's favorite brothel on Forest Park Avenue. She was often in trouble with the city over prostitution and alcohol-related infractions and once unsuccessfully petitioned the city to remove the constant police presence near her bordello; she argued they violated her constitutional rights. Traynor's life on the wrong side of the law ended in her tragic murder under suspicious circumstances (possibly an organized crime hit) in 1961.

At the start of the 1925 season, Babe Ruth had a serious stomach ailment and underwent surgery. After recovery, he was told to take better care of himself, but the temptations in St. Louis were too much for him. After arriving at the Mound City's train station in August, he forgot the doctors' prohibitions and went to Traynor's business to subject himself to the charms inside. This was beyond the pale for Yankee manager Miller Huggins, who fined Ruth $5,000 and suspended him. The reason given by Huggins was "misconduct off the field." Reporters asked Huggins if the misconduct meant drinking. He responded by saying: "Of course it means drinking.

And it means a lot of other things besides." The suspension lasted nine days before the big man and his big bat returned to the lineup.

Traynor's building does not survive. The Salvation Army owns the block, and a parking lot now occupies the specific address. The building at 4007 Forest Park Avenue is reflective of the type of structures that occupied this block during the Babe's career.

Holy Cow, Carabina!

1909 LaSalle Street

Before Harry Caray became a famous baseball broadcaster for the Cardinals, Browns, Athletics, White Sox and Cubs, he was Harry Christopher Carabina, a child growing up in the Lafayette Square neighborhood of St. Louis.

Carabina was born in 1914. His father left the family around the time of Harry's birth. There was never a relationship, and Harry knew nothing about him. His mother, Daisy, did the best she could, but a single mother at the time could not provide much. He soon was living with his Aunt Doxie and her husband in a tidy, two-story brick home on LaSalle Street. His mother remarried when he was twelve but died of pneumonia two years later.

Carabina worked from an early age, selling newspapers on street corners when he was eight. He attended elementary school on Clayton Avenue (Dewey School) and found time to play sports. His family moved to Webster Groves, and he was a good enough shortstop and second baseman for Webster Groves High to receive a scholarship offer from the University of Alabama. Fortunately for his future fans, he did not have enough money to pay room and board, so he did not accept.

A local sporting-goods company hired Carabina to work in sales, but he still wanted to be involved in baseball. In 1940, he wrote a letter to Merle Jones, general manager at KMOX, and said he was a better announcer than the current crop doing the games for the station. Jones auditioned Carabina and liked him but thought he needed experience. Jones sent him to a radio station in Joliet, Illinois. The station manager there talked him into changing his name to Caray. By 1945, he was back in St. Louis, broadcasting Cardinal games with Gabby Street.

Caray's style was popular and controversial. He was a fan in the booth, rooting for the players to do well but unafraid to criticize their poor play. He was an exciting broadcaster to listen to and a great promotor of both the game

Left: Publicity photo of Harry Caray in 1951. *Howard Earl Day*.

Right: Harry Caray's childhood home on LaSalle today. *Kathryn Flaspohler*.

and products sold by the sponsors (often beer companies). He partied with fans after games at local hot spots, increasing his popularity. In 1970, the Cardinals let him go, and he went on to national fame as the Cubs broadcaster when station WGN televised Cub games over cable. His trademark saying, "Holy cow!," uttered at an exciting moment, became famous.

The home on LaSalle remains a single-family residence. It was built in 1880, a mixture of Greek Revival and Italianate architectural styles. The surrounding neighborhood maintains its historic character.

3

1927–1947

BASEBALL LIFER

3026 Laclede Avenue

Early in the twentieth century, Sumner High School was the only Black high school in St. Louis. With Mill Creek Valley's burgeoning Black population, a high school in the neighborhood was needed. Starting in 1922, a citizens' group lobbied the St. Louis Public Schools for a new high school. They were successful, and the new school project was approved. It was given the name Vashon, after pioneering African American father and son educators, George Boyer Vashon and John Vashon.

Ground-breaking for the new school was in 1925. The building was designed by Rockwell Milligan, who, along with William Ittner, brought school design to a higher art. Over fifty school buildings in St. Louis were designed by these men. The high school opened in 1927, providing for Mill Creek Valley and surrounding neighborhoods.

Quincy Trouppe was born in Georgia in 1912. His family moved to St. Louis in 1921, seeking better opportunities than sharecropping. They settled in the Compton Heights neighborhood. Quincy attended the new Vashon High School, which was adjacent to the Negro League Stars Park. In his senior year, Vashon faced Sumner High for the city baseball championship, held in Stars Park. Trouppe met one of his heroes, James "Cool Papa" Bell, who attended the game, which Vashon won.

Left: Vashon High School, 1927. *Missouri Historical Society.*

Below: Quincy Trouppe in catcher's gear in Cuba. Willie Mays is third from the right. *National Baseball Hall of Fame and Museum.*

Trouppe went on to a lifetime in baseball. He briefly played with Bell on the pennant-winning 1931 St. Louis Stars. He played on barnstorming teams, in the Mexican League and in Venezuela, Cuba and Puerto Rico. In 1939, he joined the St. Louis Stars in the Negro American League. In 1952, he achieved a lifelong dream, playing a few games with the Cleveland Indians. His career with Cleveland was short, but he caught a couple innings pitched by Sam "Toothpick" Jones. It marked the first all-Black battery in American League history.

In 1953, Trouppe retired from playing and scouted for the St. Louis Cardinals, the first Black scout the team employed. He moved to California in the 1960s, did more scouting for St. Louis and ran a restaurant with his third wife. He wrote a book, *20 Years Too Soon*, and provided most of the footage Ken Burns used on the Negro Leagues in his *Baseball* miniseries. Trouppe relocated to St. Louis late in life and died from Alzheimer's in 1993. He is buried in Calvary Cemetery.

Vashon High School was moved in 1963 after the Mill Creek Valley clearance. Thankfully, the grand building was taken over by Harris Stowe State University, which still uses and lovingly maintains the educational palace today.

YOGI

5447 Elizabeth Avenue

On May 12, 1925, Pietro and Paulina welcomed their fourth child, Lorenzo Pietro, into the world. Pietro had immigrated to the United States in 1909. He earned enough money to bring Paulina over in 1912. They settled into St. Louis's Italian neighborhood, the Hill. The couple called their son Lawrence Peter to help him assimilate. They couldn't pronounce "Lawrence" with their accent, so he became known as "Lawdie."

Lawrence Berra, like many immigrant children, embraced the national game of baseball. His parents did not understand the game, but if he did his chores and went to school, free time was earned. He and his friends loved the movies, and he picked up another nickname when his friends thought he resembled an Indian snake charmer they saw on the big screen. Yogi stuck, and everyone, even his parents, called him that from then on.

Berra, despite his parents' objections, quit school after the eighth grade and went to work. He was fired from several jobs because he often left early to play baseball. He went to a St. Louis Cardinal tryout with his neighbor and best friend, Joe. Joe got a contract with a $500 bonus; Yogi was offered a contract but no bonus. He turned it down. The five-foot, seven-inch youngster with a lumpy body and funny running stride did not impress Cardinal management. A few months later, the New York Yankees offered a contract with a $500 bonus, and Berra signed.

That was money well spent by the Yankees. They received the best baseball player St. Louis ever produced. But before his major league career started,

Left: Yogi Berra around 1950. *Missouri Historical Society*.

Below: Berra's childhood home today. *Kathryn Flaspohler*.

Yogi served in the U.S. Navy in World War II, participating in the Normandy landings on a small landing craft missile boat. He earned a Purple Heart and two battle stars during his time in the navy.

As catcher for the dominant Yankees, Berra won ten World Series rings, three MVP awards, appeared in eighteen All-Star Games and was elected to baseball's Hall of Fame in 1972. He was a great ambassador of the game and produced many memorable quotes that sound funny but contain wisdom.

"It ain't over till it's over." Meaning, "Play hard the whole game."

"No one goes there anymore. It's too crowded." In other words, "My friends and I don't go there anymore because it is crowded with people we do not know."

"Always go to other people's funerals, otherwise they won't go to yours." Meaning, "Do the right thing in life."

His childhood home, a wood-framed bungalow built in 1923, is typical of homes in the Hill neighborhood. The home is owned by his niece, who lives there. A bronze star is set into the front sidewalk noting Yogi's years of residence.

Not the Best Player on His Street

5446 Elizabeth Avenue

Joe Garagiola, son of Italian immigrants, was born in 1926 and grew up in the Hill neighborhood of St. Louis. He chummed around with all the neighborhood kids, but a short, dumpy kid who lived across the street was his best friend. They hung out together, spending much of the time playing baseball.

At fifteen, he and his buddy tried out for the St. Louis Cardinals. The team offered Joe a contract and a $500 signing bonus. They offered his friend Yogi a contract but no bonus, so Yogi turned them down. Garagiola was only fifteen, younger than league rules allowed, so he signed the deal secretly. The Cardinals sent him to their minor league team in Springfield, Missouri, and made him the clubhouse boy. He collected towels, shined shoes, ran errands and continued to hone his baseball skills. He returned home to St. Louis after the minor league season and went back to high school. Garagiola finished high school, just in time to be drafted and serve in World War II. After the war, he made his major league debut for the Cardinals in 1946.

Right: Joe Garagiola in 1953. *Bowman Gum Company*.

Below: Garagiola's childhood home today. *Kathryn Flaspohler*.

Garagiola won a World Series ring with the 1946 team. He was an effective platoon player for the Cardinals, but just as he was coming into his own, he suffered a serious shoulder separation in a 1950 collision with Jackie Robinson. He missed three months, and the injury bothered him the rest of his undistinguished career. He spent limited time with Pittsburgh, the Chicago Cubs and the New York Giants before retiring at age twenty-eight.

Garagiola was blessed with the gift of gab and embarked on a long career as a broadcaster, show host and after-dinner speaker. He was a partner to Harry Caray for a time on the Cardinal broadcasts, hosted NBC's *The Today Show* in two different stints, guest-hosted for Johnny Carson, emceed game shows and hosted the Westminster Dog Show for nine years. In his spare time, he wrote three best-selling baseball books. One of his favorite lines when he did speaking events was, "Most major league players were the best in their town. I wasn't even the best player on my street!"

Garagiola gave back to the game, founding the Baseball Assistance Team, which helped former players in financial need. He crusaded against the use of chewing tobacco, giving talks to major league players on the dangers of smokeless tobacco. Curt Schilling, among others, credited him with helping him quit chewing.

The house he grew up in, across the street from Yogi Berra's home, is still a private residence. There are two stars in the sidewalk in front of the home. One shows Joe's years of residence. The other is for his locally famous brother Mickey.

Muscles Does *Not* Walk Like a Duck

11735 Denny Road

For seven seasons, starting in 1933, Joe Medwick's powerful bat led the St. Louis Cardinals' Gashouse Gang's offense. He was a high-average doubles machine, raking line drives to all fields while in the middle of the lineup. During this stretch, he averaged 49 doubles a season, hit .335 during his Cardinal career and won a Most Valuable Player award in 1937, the same year he led the league in home runs, batting average and runs batted in.

Medwick was a surly teammate, involved in well-publicized disagreements over such matters as taking too much time in the batting cage and being eclipsed by another player when a photographer was taking his picture. He did not endear himself to the media, either, frequently snubbing them when they were looking for a quote.

Medwick's attitude was shaped while on the Gashouse Gang. The group of colorful characters, led by Dizzy Dean and Pepper Martin, was long on horseplay but also competitive. Once they found a weakness in someone, they exploited it. Medwick's weakness was a propensity to waddle when

Joe Medwick during the 1934 World Series. *State Historical Society of Missouri.*

he walked. Teammates started calling him "Ducky," and as soon as Joe expressed his displeasure, they ratcheted up the attacks.

According to Bob Broeg, one day against the Pittsburgh Pirates, Joe was in left field while Dizzy Dean was pitching with the bases loaded. A dying quail was hit near the left-field line. Medwick, whose defense was best described as indifferent, let the ball fall untouched while the bases cleared. After the inning, Dean complained about Ducky's effort. Dizzy's brother Paul joined the complaining, and they headed toward Medwick on the bench. Joe grabbed a bat and yelled, "Step right up, boys, and I'll separate you brothers." An inning later, Medwick hit a grand slam to give St. Louis the lead, filled his mouth at the water cooler and spat on Dean's shoes. "All right you big meathead, there's your three runs back and one extra. Let's see you hold the damned lead." This incident, while not documented in a box score, was a perfect tale highlighting the Gashouse Gang's reputation.

Medwick much preferred the nickname "Muscles," and most of his teammates began using that instead of the hated "Ducky"—if for no other reason than to avoid tangling with the bulky Hungarian from New Jersey.

Branch Rickey, following his philosophy that it is better to get rid of a player a year too early than a year too late, traded Medwick to Brooklyn in 1940 for four players and a large bundle of cash. Six days later, while facing the Cardinals, he was beaned. The Cardinal pitcher insisted it was an accident, but who knows? Fortunately, he recovered from the concussion and fashioned a seventeen-year career.

Medwick mellowed in retirement and was elected to the Hall of Fame in 1968 after enough writers had either forgotten or forgiven the rudeness Muscles showed toward them. He died of a heart attack in 1975 during spring training while

A fan paying his respects to Medwick. *Brian Flaspohler.*

doing some batting instruction for the Cardinals. He is buried in St. Lucas Cemetery on Denny Road (N38° 32.246', W90° 23.322'). This United Church of Christ cemetery was founded in 1880 and contains one other major league player, Bill Byerly.

Hall of Famer? Check the Night Shift

2101 Lucas and Hunt Road

James Nichols was born near Starkville, Mississippi, in 1903. His dad died months before he was born, but his mom married Jonas Bell after James was born. He and his seven siblings all worked on the family farm. James learned to play baseball when recreation was allowed.

When Nichols was seventeen, he moved to St. Louis and lived with four of his brothers. He got a job in a packinghouse and changed his surname to Bell. For recreation, he played ball with the Compton Hill Cubs. In 1922, his Cubs faced the Negro League St. Louis Stars in an exhibition game. They lost, 9–2, but Bell impressed the Stars, striking out nine of them, so the Stars signed him.

The Stars began using Bell as a pitcher. He was effective and picked up the nickname "Cool" for his ability to pitch well under pressure. His teammates added "Papa" later, purely because they thought it sounded better. His running speed was noticed immediately. During his rookie season, he raced and won easily against Jimmie Lyons, the fastest player in the Negro Leagues. In later years, Satchel Paige said of Bell, "He was so fast, he could turn off the light and hop into bed before it got dark."

The Stars soon decided that Bell's amazing speed and capable bat were more suited to the outfield. Starting in 1925, he had a five-year stretch in which he led the league in stolen bases four times, runs scored three times and doubles once, and he never batted below .313. Bell, along with teammates Willie Wells and Mule Suttles, led St. Louis to three pennants and two league championships in 1928, 1930 and 1931. The Negro National League folded after the 1931 season, and Bell embarked on the second phase of his career, playing for the Pittsburgh Crawfords in the second Negro National League. That team won three pennants in four years with Bell in center field and batting first.

After his twenty-five-year playing career ended in 1946, he retired to St. Louis with his wife, Clara. They lived in a small apartment on Dickson Street, and he worked at City Hall as a night watchman. He attended Cardinal games occasionally and anonymously. However, in 1974, the special committee for Negro Leaguers elected him to the Baseball Hall of Fame, the fifth Negro League player so honored. St. Louis renamed Dickson Street as James "Cool Papa" Bell Avenue.

Top: James "Cool Papa" Bell. *National Baseball Hall of Fame and Museum.*

Bottom: Bell's impressive gravestone. *Kathryn Flaspohler.*

Bell traveled to Cooperstown for the Hall of Fame ceremony every year after that, staying to greet fans, accommodating everyone no matter how long it took. He was modest about his abilities but proud of his achievements. He and Clara stayed in their small apartment the rest of their lives. She passed in January 1991, and he died two months later. They were survived by daughter Connie. Bell's epitaph reflects his belief that his life was a blessing: "I did the best I could with what I had." Their grave (N38° 41.242' W90° 17.673') is in St. Peter's Cemetery on Lucas and Hunt Road, as are those of several other major league players. The Bells' apartment on Cool Papa Bell Avenue has been demolished and replaced with new construction.

FAIRGROUNDS HOTEL

3644 Natural Bridge Avenue

The epicenter of baseball activity in St. Louis was once the area surrounding Fairgrounds Park in north city. Sportsman's Park, home of the St. Louis Cardinals and the St. Louis Browns, was six short blocks to the southwest. Two high schools were within walking distance. Getting downtown was easy by bus or trolley. This activity demanded a hotel nearby.

Fairgrounds Hotel, designed by architect J.T. Craven and built by Boaz-Kiel Construction Company, is a late nineteenth- and twentieth-century revival-style building, completed in 1928. It opened as a luxury hotel, one of two hotels serving the area near Fairgrounds Park. Mentioned in its grand opening advertisements were such enticements as "a shower and tub in every room" and "$1 Sunday dinners." The bottom floor of the hotel offered a restaurant, tavern and retail amenities. Soon after opening, the hotel converted some of its rooms into small apartments, providing hotel services to the apartment residents.

The hotel was popular with St. Louis Browns and St. Louis Cardinals players who didn't maintain permanent residence in St. Louis. The proximity to Sportsman's Park and the bus and trolley lines meant a player did not need a car. Documentation of which players stayed there and when is scant, as city directories listed only permanent city residents. However, Cardinals manager Gabby Street rented apartment 601 in 1933. This detail is known because a crime report in a local paper reported twelve dollars stolen from his trousers.

Stan Musial, with his wife, Lil, moved into the Fairgrounds Hotel in late 1941. Musial's biography notes that many single ball players lived in the hotel during the baseball season. Musial stayed in the hotel until 1948, when

Right: An ad for the Fairgrounds Hotel in 1935. St. Louis Globe-Democrat.

Below: The Fairground Apartments today. *Kathryn Flaspohler*.

he bought a home in South St. Louis. Musial won the National League's Most Valuable Player Award in 1943 and led St. Louis to a World Series victory while staying at the hotel. It was a popular place for local fans to catch a glimpse of their favorite players before and after games.

The eight-story building's exterior is largely unchanged today. After the Cardinals moved to their downtown stadium in 1966, demand for hotel rooms around Fairgrounds Park evaporated. The building was converted into a senior living center, then in 2001, it was converted into an apartment complex. Now known as the Fairgrounds Park Place Apartments, it still offers retail space on the ground floor with apartment living next to Fairgrounds Park.

RICKEY DOES SOME FARMING

5405 Bartmer Avenue

Wesley Branch Rickey had a short major league career but set a record that still stands today. In 1907, while a member of the New York Yankees, he allowed 13 stolen bases by the Washington Senators. "My arm was numb and I was helpless to do anything," Rickey explained. He hit a paltry .182 for the season, and his playing career, aside from two pinch-hit appearances in 1914, was over.

Rickey was a Bible-toting Republican Methodist; a teetotaler who wouldn't play or manage on Sundays; a man who never cursed more than an exasperated, "Judas Priest!" He was a shrewd judge of baseball talent and a harsh negotiator in the off-season. In 1932, Jim Bottomley held out for a $15,000 salary, which Rickey finally agreed to late in the spring. Bottomley reported late to the spring training site and missed the early part of the season while getting in shape. Rickey docked him $2,100 for the missed games.

Rickey began in the St. Louis Browns' front office, but the Cardinals, appreciating his skills, lured him to their executive suite. When Sam Breadon became owner, he and Rickey became an unlikely but effective team. Rickey had amazing outside-the-box ideas. Breadon had the vision to figure out which were most cost effective.

Rickey's most transformative idea was for a major league team to buy minor league teams and use those teams to develop talent specifically for the big league club. Breadon loved the idea but needed money. He sold Robison Field and moved the Cardinals into Sportsman's Park as tenants of the St. Louis Browns. The proceeds from the sale paid off the team's debts and allowed them to buy stakes in a few minor league clubs. No longer would these teams be independent and sell their players to the highest bidder. Over the years, the Cardinals expanded their minor league system, owning more than a dozen teams at their peak. The minor league teams, loaded with talent found by Rickey, sent players to the Cardinals, turning the team from a perennial cellar dweller to a world champion in 1926.

Branch Rickey in 1920. *University of Michigan Library Digital Collections.*

Rickey's home today. *Kathryn Flaspohler.*

Rickey's other innovations included sandpits to help players learn to slide, string frame strike zones for pitching practice and tees to allow players to hone their swing. While he developed the innovative Cardinals' farm system, he lived with his wife and five daughters in a home on Bartmer. The neighborhood is a mile and a half from Sportsman's Park, where Rickey spent his eighty-hour workweeks. They lived here in the 1920s and 1930s, moving to a Clayton Road address by 1940. Most homes on the street are historic from the period, with many built in the late 1890s. Rickey's home on Bartmer Avenue, erected in 1911, is vacant today and needs maintenance and restoration.

THE WHISTLE BLOWS, THE KID ROLLS

2325 Sublette Avenue

The shrill whistle of the plant sounding the end of the shift let young Lawrence know he needed to drop what he was doing (frequently playing baseball) and hightail it to Sublette Avenue to take care of the most important chore of the day. Lawrence, known as Yogi to everyone, didn't mind chores.

He was often recruited for chores at his Italian neighborhood home, and he sold newspapers in the mornings at the busy intersection of Vandeventer, Kingshighway and Shenandoah before heading to Shaw Elementary School.

After school, Yogi met up with his friend Joe and others to play baseball. When the whistle sounded, the youngster ran over to Joe Fassi's and picked up a bucket of beer. It was a neighborhood race, because all the kids had the same job. They fought for position when getting to Fassi's, trying to get in Emil Fassi's line, because he poured beer with less foam.

After getting his bucket filled, Yogi hustled the short distance home, aiming to have the bucket sitting on the kitchen table before his dad, Pietro, finished walking home. The Italian family patriarch wanted his bucket of beer to accompany supper after a hard day's labor. More times than not, Yogi got the beer home before his dad got there.

In 1926, Paul Fassi started a grocery business in a building he constructed on Sublette Avenue. His five sons—Joe, Louis, Vince, Emil and Paul—and their spouses worked in the business. After Paul retired, Joe took over and switched the business to a tavern and restaurant. He renamed the tavern Joe

Joe Fassi's Tavern in the 1940s, with a neighborhood boy waiting for the whistle. *Tom Coll.*

Joe Fassi Sausage and Sandwich Factory today. *Kathryn Flaspohler.*

Fassi's. The Italian food on the menu was straight from the mind of Paul's wife, Mama Rosie. The business thrived over the years. Joe Fassi died in 1986, but younger brother Vince kept the business going until 1992, when grandson Tom Coll took over operations. Tom reimagined the business as a sandwich factory, and it continues to this day.

The family owns the entire building, using half of it for the sandwich shop and leasing the other section to another business. It is a great place to stop for lunch, serving generous portions of both hot and cold Italian sandwiches in a space with walls covered with photos and stories of the place's history.

The Cat Finds His Mouse

1204 South McKnight Road

In 1937, Johnny Mize, in the middle of his second season with the St. Louis Cardinals, was scorching the league with his lumber. The handsome Mize broke many female fans' hearts on the morning of August 8. He married Jene Adams, a St. Louis native. The couple took no time off for a honeymoon. In fact, the afternoon after the wedding, he played in a doubleheader against the Philadelphia Phillies. He went 2 for 9 in the twin bill, lowering his season average to .362. But marriage did not negatively impact his hitting in the long run. For the season, his batting average was a robust .364.

Mize, a Georgia native, had baseball blood. He was a distant cousin of Ty Cobb; another distant cousin, Clara Merritt, married Babe Ruth. The left-handed-hitting, right-handed-throwing first baseman fashioned a Hall of Fame career playing for the St. Louis Cardinals, New York Giants and New York Yankees.

The "Big Cat," nicknamed for his work around first base, was most known for his bat. The easygoing big man played six seasons for the Cardinals, finishing second in the Most Valuable Player race twice and leading the league in home runs twice and in batting average once. The Cardinals traded him to the Giants four days after the Pearl Harbor attack for three journeymen and $50,000. This was another move Rickey made to bolster his personal income, as he received a percentage from every player sale.

Mize continued his good play, spraying line drives to all fields. He clubbed 359 home runs in his fifteen-year career while striking out just 524 times.

Johnny Mize admiring one of his prodigious blasts. *National Baseball Hall of Fame.*

The Adams home today. *Kathryn Flaspohler.*

All of this was achieved while missing three full seasons serving in the navy during World War II. In retirement, Mize lived in Georgia and Florida, played golf and signed autographs for everyone who asked. After a thirty-year wait due to baseball writers' impressions of his poor defense, he was elected to the Baseball Hall of Fame in 1981.

During his playing days, Johnny and Jene maintained a permanent residence in his hometown of Demorest, Georgia, but while playing for the Cardinals from 1937 to 1941, the couple lived with Jene's parents in a Richmond Heights home during the season. The home on South McKnight Road, built in the mid-1930s for the Adams family, is an attractive, two-story wood-frame structure. Richmond Heights is an inner-ring suburb adjacent to St. Louis, southwest of Forest Park. The home remains a single-family residence today.

HEINE MEINE'S LABOR OF LOVE

153 Lemay Ferry Road

Henry Meine was born in 1896 in Carondolet, an unincorporated area south of St. Louis. He was forced to grow up fast in the German neighborhood, because his father died of pneumonia when Meine was fourteen. He apprenticed as a blacksmith, following his father's trade.

During World War I, Heine—the nickname given to many ethnic Germans named Henry—served in the cavalry and played baseball. While serving, he developed a spitball and became an effective pitcher. After returning home, he took over operation of the tavern his deceased cousin had owned and played semipro ball around the St. Louis area to great effect. The tavern business was impacted when Prohibition passed in 1920, so when a St. Louis Browns scout signed him, he was happy to play ball for a living.

The spitballing Meine had another unpleasant surprise ahead. Major League Baseball banned the spitball beginning in 1921. He pitched in the minors in 1921 using his spitball but after that season was forced to learn how to pitch without his primary weapon. He was successful enough to earn a brief call-up to the Browns in 1922, consisting of one four-inning appearance. He continued in the minor leagues, but his results were inconsistent. He retired after the 1926 season.

Meine returned to operate his "soda shop," actually a speakeasy, during Prohibition, but his customers urged him to try baseball again. He returned to the minor leagues in 1928, and his contract was purchased by the Pittsburgh Pirates for the 1929 season. The thirty-three-year-old, no longer using a spitball openly, fashioned an effective six-year career with the Pirates, including winning 19 games (tying two other pitchers for the league lead) in 1931. He retired on his own terms and went back to the tavern. With Prohibition repealed, he was now able to sell alcohol.

Heine Meine did not leave the game he loved. He built a baseball field

across the street from his tavern, doing all the upkeep himself. He opened a baseball school and hired former professional players as instructors, including Vern Stephens and Marty McManus. He led squads of "old-timers," former major league players such as Johnny Tobin and Joe Medwick, against local teams. He recruited position players so he could always pitch for the team. His field became the epicenter for baseball in South St. Louis, and he remained active in amateur baseball until his death in 1968 from cancer.

A Heine Meine baseball card from 1933. *Goudey Gum Company.*

Heine Meine Field, now owned by the Hancock Place School District, is active

Cardinals Care sign at Heine Meine Field. *Kathryn Flaspohler.*

today. Little League games as well as high school, American Legion and community college games have been played there. It hosted the Missouri State High School Championship game five times, including in 1966 and 1967, when a young Jerry Reuss led Ritenour High School to the title. The St. Louis Cardinals' charitable arm, Cardinals Care, helped fund a $500,000 renovation in 2012, improving the fields and updating the facilities.

HOLLOCHER'S END

2307 South Lindbergh Boulevard

On August 14, 1940, around 8:00 a.m., Constable Arthur Mosely and Deputy Constable Charles Gordon noticed a car parked in a driveway off Lindbergh Boulevard leading to an abandoned house. They discovered a body with a self-inflected wound in the neck and a newly purchased shotgun. The price tag was still attached to the gun. Other evidence included a pair of sunglasses and a membership card of the Association of Professional Baseball Players. A note was on the car dashboard: "Call Walnut-4123, Mrs. Ruth Hollocher." The constables recognized the deceased as Charlie Hollocher, well known in St. Louis.

Hollocher was a baseball phenom who grew up in St. Louis and played on amateur and semiprofessional teams in the area until he was scouted and signed by the minor league Keokuk, Iowa Indians. After three seasons in the minor leagues, the slick-fielding, twenty-two-year-old's contract was purchased by the Chicago Cubs, who put him to work in the Windy City in 1918 as the team's starting shortstop.

Hollocher played seven solid seasons with the Cubs, compiled a lifetime batting average of .304 and cultivated a reputation as an above-average defensive shortstop. However, he only played half of each of his last two seasons, complaining of stomach ailments. He saw many doctors, but none of them could bring him any relief or even diagnose his complaint. After the 1924 season, he retired from baseball, no longer able to play due to his illness.

After baseball, Hollocher worked various jobs, including as a scout for the Cubs, an investigator for a county prosecutor and a night watchman. Later, he opened a tavern on the corner of Dale Avenue and Hawthorne Place in Richmond Heights. His tavern building still exists but is now an office. He and his first wife divorced, and he married Ruth about a year

Charlie Hollocher. *Library of Congress.*

The exit of St. Joseph's, the approximate location of Charlie Hollocher's suicide. *Kathryn Flaspohler*.

before his suicide. She noted later that he was often depressed about his stomach ailments.

St. Joseph's Acadamy, a Catholic girls' high school built in 1955, now stands near the location where Hollocher's body was found by the policemen.

ROOMIES SOUTHWORTH AND SEWELL

3745 Lindell Boulevard

The Lindell Towers apartment buildings, located in midtown, were designed by architect Preston Bradshaw. The East Tower was built in 1927, the West Tower in 1928. These fashionable apartments provided housing near Sportsman's Park, which served as home field for the St. Louis Browns and the St. Louis Cardinals.

During the 1944 season, Cardinals manager Billy Southworth and Browns manager Luke Sewell shared an apartment in the West Tower. Both teams played their home games in Sportsman's Park, so the baseball schedule always had one team at home while the other was on the road.

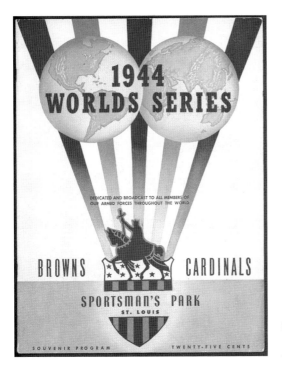

Souvenir program from the
1944 World Series. *Missouri
Historical Society.*

It was a perfect arrangement for both men, since there was no conflict for the use of the apartment. Effectively, each had his own place. Sewell's wife and two daughters joined him when the Browns were home, vacating the apartment and heading back to their home in Ohio when he left on a road trip.

At the beginning of the season, the St. Louis Cardinals were the favorite to win the National League pennant and advance to the World Series. In 1942 and 1943, the team won 106 and 105 games, respectively, winning the World Series against the New York Yankees in 1942, although losing the rematch in 1943. If anything, the team exceeded expectations, winning 105 games. The Pittsburgh Pirates stayed close until September but went on a losing streak, and the Cardinals breezed to the finish, winning the NL pennant by fourteen and a half games.

The American League was a big surprise. Many major league teams lost players to military service in World War II; 1944 saw the departure of large numbers of players. The St. Louis Browns lost fewer than most. In 1943, the team finished sixth in the eight-team AL, but they reversed course in 1944. After an exciting pennant race, culminating in the Browns' four-game sweep of the Yankees in their last series of the year, they won

Lindell Tower West today. *Kathryn Flaspohler.*

89 games and the team's only pennant in their history in St. Louis, edging the Detroit Tigers by one game.

This turn of events meant that the managers would both be at their apartment for the World Series! Opposing managers sharing a room after each game just would not work. How would they resolve this? One apocryphal story is that they flipped a coin. Sewell won the toss, so he stayed in the apartment. The truth is that Southworth telegraphed Sewell before the Browns' last game against New York. In the missive, Billy wished Luke luck, said the Browns would win and told Sewell to keep the apartment for the World Series.

A neighbor went out of town during the Series and offered his apartment to Southworth, so both men still stayed in the Lindell Towers. Southworth's generosity was karmically rewarded, as the Cardinals defeated the Browns in the World Series, four games to two.

Both towers remain as apartments. They underwent extensive interior renovations in 2003, but the exterior of the buildings reflect what they looked like in 1944.

IS A BASEBALL'S TERMINAL VELOCITY FATAL?

10 North Tucker Boulevard

The year was 1908. There was no Internet, television or radio. People had to create their own entertainment. Two Washington Senator fans offered $500 to a person who could catch a ball thrown from the top of the Washington Monument. There was rampant speculation about how fast a ball would travel after falling from such a height. Would it be fast enough to kill?

The Washington Senators' Charles Street was in the middle of his first full season with the team and was not making much money. The prize money represented a significant bonus for the young catcher. And he routinely caught Walter Johnson's fastball, so a ball dropped from the Washington Monument surely would not travel much faster. After the proper permits were received, the two fans brought a bucket of balls to the top of the obelisk. They threw the balls from a window 550 feet above ground level, and Street, using a regulation catcher's mitt but wearing street clothes, snagged the fifteenth one dropped, collecting the wager. He suffered no ill effects, catching a game pitched by Johnson later the same day.

Left: Civil Courts Building in the 1940s. *Missouri Historical Society*.

Right: Civil Courts Building today. *Kathryn Flaspohler*.

Street finished his seven-year major league career with a reputation as a good-fielding, no-hitting receiver. The nickname "Gabby" was bestowed on him for his proclivity to talk at length. He managed the St. Louis Cardinals for three and a half seasons, winning two pennants and a World Series. But his gift of gab was more useful for the new medium of radio. He landed a job as a radio color commentator for St. Louis Browns games and then for Cardinal games.

Thirty-seven years after his Washington, D.C. stunt, the sixty-two-year-old Street was asked to duplicate his feat by catching a ball thrown from the St. Louis Civil Courts Building for a war bond rally. He agreed, showing up with a catcher's mitt and in street clothes, just as in 1908. His rookie broadcast partner, Harry Caray, was the designated thrower. The *St. Louis Star-Times* and *St. Louis Post-Dispatch* reported that Street caught two of three balls Caray dropped. Griesedieck Brewery, Street's radio broadcast sponsor, bought $300,000 in war bonds to acquire the second baseball Street caught, and $100,000 was raised by the sale of other baseball memorabilia.

The 380-foot-tall, art deco Civil Courts Building was designed by a commission of eight architecture and two engineering firms. It was constructed from 1926 to 1930, funded by a voter-approved $83 million bond issue designed to erect a series of "monumental" buildings around Memorial Plaza. The new building replaced the historic Old Courthouse. The bond issue covered $4 million of the construction, while the city paid an additional $1 million to cover overruns. At the time of its dedication, it was reported to be the tallest courthouse in the world. The pyramid at the top of the building, supported by thirty-two Ionic columns, resembles the Turkish Mausoleum at Halicarnassus. The Civil Courts Building still serves its original function today.

Neat Feat, Street

A local paper showing Gabby Street's catch. St. Louis Star-Times, *May 25, 1945.*

GIRLS PLAY BALL, TOO

10180 Gravois Road

Erma Bergmann, born in St. Louis in 1924, had a pioneering spirit. Her mother wanted her to take piano lessons, but she played ball with her two brothers instead. She attended McKinley High School, which had limited sports programs for girls, so she played in softball leagues and, ignoring common convention, played for the St. Louis Phantoms, a boys' baseball team. She won ten games while pitching for the team.

In 1943, there was real concern that World War II would interrupt professional baseball. Many players were drafted, and gas rationing meant limited transportation. Chicago Cubs owner Philip Wrigley decided that a professional women's league could help fill the baseball gap. He and a handful of other entrepreneurs founded the All-American Girls Baseball League. The teams were in Michigan, Illinois, Indiana and Wisconsin during the twelve years the league existed.

Right: Policewoman Erma Bergmann. *St. Louis Metropolitan Police Department.*

Below: Sunset Memorial Park chapel and mausoleum. *Kathryn Flaspohler.*

The league's talent scouts recruited women from amateur softball ranks. Bergmann was playing fast-pitch softball in St. Louis and impressed the league scouts. She was signed to play for the Muskegon Lassies in 1946.

Bergmann played six seasons in the league for various teams. Initially, she pitched underhanded, but the league rules changed over time to mirror baseball rules. She successfully transitioned to side-arm pitching, then full overhand pitching, one of the few pitchers in the league to throw all three styles.

While Erma played for bad teams, she was a good pitcher. She hurled a no-hitter against the Grand Rapids Chicks in 1947. Her career ERA was a very good 2.54 in her six seasons; she hit a less-impressive .201. Her career highlight was a game against the Rockford Peaches in her rookie season. She hit her only career home run in the top of the ninth and blanked the Peaches in the bottom of the ninth to win the game with her parents in attendance.

After her baseball career ended, she worked as a clerk for the City of St. Louis. She got a job as a police officer in 1956, one of only a handful of female officers on the force. She served twenty-five years on the police force with an exemplary record.

After retirement, she became a vocal ambassador for women in baseball. Some of her memorabilia is on display in the Baseball Hall of Fame, and she was active in league reunions. On her ninetieth birthday, she threw out the first pitch before a Cardinals game.

Bergmann died at the age of ninety-one on September 13, 2015. She is buried in Sunset Memorial Park cemetery on Gravois Road (N38° 32.671', W90° 20.674'). There are a handful of other baseball luminaries buried in this cemetery, including Cardinal owner August "Gussie" Busch (N38° 32.903', W90° 20.532') and longtime *St. Louis Post-Dispatch* writer Bob Broeg (N38° 32.889', W90° 20.515').

BEAUMONT HIGH'S HALL OF FAMER

4713 Northland Avenue

Beaumont High School counts fourteen Major League Baseball players among its alumni, but one famous graduate is a baseball Hall of Famer who never played in the major leagues.

Earl Sydney Weaver grew up in a modest two-family home on Northland Avenue. His father owned a dry-cleaning business on Grand Boulevard near Sportsman's Park. The St. Louis Cardinals and St. Louis Browns were among

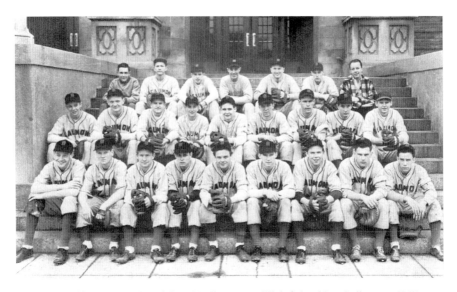

Earl Weaver *(front row, center)* and the 1947 Beaumont High School baseball team. *1947 Beaumont High School yearbook.*

his clients. He brought young Earl with him when he would do pickups and deliveries, letting the youngster explore the Sportsman's Park clubhouses and play on the field. Baseball ran in Weaver's blood early.

Despite his size, Weaver was a three-sport athlete for Beaumont, playing football, basketball and baseball. Missouri did not sponsor a state high school baseball tournament until 1950, but Beaumont was a powerful team in the 1940s. With Weaver holding down second base, the team won the city championship in 1946 and finished second in 1947.

The Cardinals and the Browns each offered Weaver a contract. He signed with the Cardinals for $1,500. The Browns offered $2,000 but required that he stay in the minors to get paid. Earl took the no-strings-attached money. He toiled in the Cardinals' minor league system for six seasons, never batting higher than .282, then played three seasons in the Pittsburgh Pirates' system, performing no better.

The Baltimore Orioles picked him up in 1957, more as a manager than as a player. He managed in Baltimore's minor league system for eleven seasons, working up from the lowest-level team in the D League to the AAA affiliate. His teams won at every level, and at thirty-seven, he became manager of the Baltimore Orioles.

The fiery Weaver was a very successful major league manager. He was the bane of AL umpires, garnering 96 regular-season ejections in his career,

Weaver's childhood home sat in this vacant lot. *Kathryn Flaspohler.*

fourth most in history. He had particular issues with umpire Ron Luciano, whom Weaver felt was both a showoff and didn't get into position to make correct calls. There was no question in the dugout that the diminutive Weaver was the boss. He often got into shouting matches with his players but never backed down. The combativeness worked for him. In seventeen major league seasons, his teams won four AL pennants and the World Series in 1970. The only losing team Weaver managed was his last, in 1986. After that season, he retired to Florida.

His childhood home is gone. Next to the now-vacant lot is a home that was contemporary with Weaver's. The area is now, as it was then, a working-class neighborhood.

MAYA ANGELOU'S NEIGHBOR

3216 Chouteau Avenue

The New York Yankees' long history of success is due, in part, to their stability at the catcher position. From 1929 to 1966, with a short break during and immediately after World War II, they had just three men catch the majority of their games each season: Bill Dickey, Yogi Berra and Elston

Left: Elston Howard in 1968. *Arnie Lee.*

Below: The historic Vashon High School building today. *Kathryn Flaspohler.*

Howard. This might be the longest period of high quality for any team at any position in baseball history.

Howard was born in 1929 in St. Louis. His mother, a dietician, raised him by herself until her marriage in 1934. The family lived on Chouteau Avenue, at the southern edge of the Mill Creek Valley neighborhood. Howard, raised to have a strong work ethic, attended Toussaint L'Ouverture Elementary School. His mother also made sure his spiritual life was taken care of by regular attendance at the Mount Zion Baptist Church. Reverend Jeremiah Baker, the church pastor, was his godfather. Maya Angelou, born in 1928, lived two blocks away.

After graduating grade school, Howard attended Vashon High School. He was a four-sport star, playing and starring on Vashon's basketball, football, track and baseball teams. Before Missouri had integrated basketball championships, he led the Vashon team to the Negro state championship in 1947 and 1948.

Several colleges offered athletic scholarships, including three Big Ten schools. The Kansas City Monarchs went to Howard's mom and negotiated a contract for him to play in the Negro Leagues. He played a single season with Kansas City before being sold to the New York Yankees. After serving in the army during the Korean War and spending three seasons in the minor leagues, he debuted with the Yankees in 1955, their first African American player. He played more outfield than catcher due to Berra's presence on the team, but in 1960, at the tender age of thirty-one, he became the number-one receiver. For his fifteen-year career, he was named to twelve All-Star Games, received two Gold Gloves as catcher and won the American League Most Valuable Player Award in 1963.

Little historical evidence remains of Howard's neighborhood. His home was demolished in the 1970s. The elementary school was torn down in the early 1960s. Vashon High School's building still stands as part of Harris Stowe State University.

The First Modern Sports Bar

3701 Sullivan Avenue

A neighborhood tavern sits at the corner of Sullivan and Spring, outside what used to be the left-field gates of Sportsman's Park. This nondescript building has a history entwined with St. Louis baseball.

Paul and Mary Palermo bought the two-story brick building in 1923 and started a dry-goods store and restaurant. In addition, Paul made homemade wine in the back that came to be in high demand during Prohibition. In conjunction with the business, named Palermo's, the family operated the first hot dog stand outside the ballpark, selling a small dog for a nickel and large one for a dime. Ballplayers frequented the establishment, because the cigarettes and chewing tobacco were cheaper than what was offered in the clubhouse.

In 1933, as soon as Prohibition was repealed, Paul converted a portion of the business to a tavern and served the baseball crowds and the bustling neighborhood. The business was profitable enough that the family opened four more taverns around the city.

Due to Paul's age and declining health, his sons Joe and Jimmy took over Palermo's after World War II. In the late 1940s, Jimmy was given a number of large posters of Browns players. He hung them in the bar. More pictures followed, but what made this the first modern sports bar was the installation of a state-of-the-art, twelve-inch Farnsworth TV in 1947. Now patrons could watch sports while enjoying a cold Griesedieck beer.

After a major renovation in the early 1950s, the interior featured game-used equipment, particularly hundreds of cracked bats, from all sixteen Major League Baseball teams. Freddie Buchholz, a batboy for both the Cardinals and Browns, was the source of much of this memorabilia. When the Cardinals were purchased by August Busch II, the house beer was

Palermo's (*circled*) on this Sportsman's Park aerial view. *Missouri Historical Society.*

Sit & Sip Lounge today. *Kathryn Flaspohler.*

changed to Budweiser. Gussie and his entourage visited the bar several times. By 1956, the bar had three TVs along with pool, shuffleboard and pinball games.

The business boomed through the 1950s. With Carter Carburetor working twenty-four hours a day and two teams using Sportsman's Park, the business served people day and night. When the new Busch Memorial Stadium opened in 1966, it marked the end of the sports bar. The family sold the business that year, collected the memorabilia from the interior and moved to Florida.

The building is still a neighborhood bar but no longer retains a sports theme.

1948–1974

Musial Becomes a St. Louisian

5447 Childress Avenue

The greatest Cardinal of them all, Stan Musial, after five full seasons with the team, winning two NL Most Valuable Player Awards and three World Series, decided he was secure enough in his job to buy a home. He and his wife, Lil, bought a modest ranch home in a newly developed South St. Louis neighborhood. They moved their son and daughter, Dick and Gerry, into the new home early in 1948. The size of this house points out the modest income that players, even stars such as Musial, received before the era of free agency.

Owning his own home sat well with Mr. Musial. In 1948, he had one of the greatest seasons in baseball history. He led the league with a .376 batting average, a .450 on-base percentage, a .702 slugging average, 131 RBIs, 230 hits, 46 doubles and 18 triples. Had he hit one more home run, he would have tied for the league lead in that category and won the NL Triple Crown. He did win his third Most Valuable Player Award, even though St. Louis finished in second place.

Musial was often seen in the neighborhood, mowing his own grass and playing with the neighborhood kids. From 1948 until 1955, he lived on Childress and continued to build his legacy as the greatest Cardinal of all time. His average season over those years was a .342 batting average, 32 home runs, 114 RBIs, 118 runs scored, a .434 on-base percentage and a

Stan and Lil Musial with their children Dick and Gerry in 1946. *Harley Hammerman/Lost Tables.*

The Musial home on Childress Avenue today. *Kathryn Flaspohler.*

.608 slugging percentage. Stan and Lil added two more daughters, Janet and Jean, to the family while living in the home.

In 1955, the family of six moved to a larger house on Westway Road for the remainder of Musial's remarkable playing career. After his retirement from baseball, they moved to Trent Road in Ladue and stayed at that address the rest of their lives. Musial spent a lifetime building goodwill with Cardinal fans and is the most beloved figure associated with the team. Lil, Stan's high school sweetheart, died in 2012 after the couple was married for seventy-two years. Stan followed a year later in 2013.

Musial's home on Childress Avenue remains a single-family residence in the St. Louis Hills neighborhood.

MAJOR LEAGUE HIGH SCHOOL

3836 Natural Bridge Avenue

Rockwell Milligan designed the majestic Beaumont High School building that today sits silently next to Natural Bridge Avenue and across from Fairgrounds Park. The impressive structure was built on the site of Robison Field, the park that served as the St. Louis Cardinals' home from 1893 to 1920. Beaumont High followed up that baseball legacy by generating an impressive number of alumni who went on to play in the major leagues.

In 1920, the Cardinals moved out of Robison Field. They became a tenant of the St. Louis Browns. Thus began a thirty-three-year period during which both the Cardinals and the Browns played in Sportsman's Park. Owner Sam

Beaumont High School in the 1920s. *Missouri Historical Society.*

Beaumont High School. *Kathryn Flaspohler.*

Breadon sold the dilapidated park to the St. Louis Public School District for desperately needed funds.

The school district, recognizing a need for a high school for the surrounding growing population, built Beaumont High on the property. The school opened in 1926, and there was plenty of baseball magic left over from the Cardinals. The school produced fifteen future major league players from 1933 to 1954. This ranks Beaumont among the top fifteen high schools all-time for most major league alumni. The most prominent of the players were starting pitcher Roy Sievers, relief pitcher Bob Miller, outfielder Pete Reiser, outfielder and first baseman Lee Thomas and outfielder Don Mueller. Sievers, with the Browns, and Miller, on the Cardinals, were lucky enough to be able to play for the hometown teams.

Other baseball talent at Beaumont included Earl Weaver, who failed to make the majors as a player but had a Hall of Fame career as manager of the Baltimore Orioles. Player and Hall of Fame manager Dick Williams attended Beaumont for one year before his family moved to California. Former major leaguer Tom Stanton taught and coached at Beaumont for several years.

With this stellar baseball talent, Beaumont was a powerhouse in the St. Louis Public High League in the 1940s and 1950s. The school won the

Missouri State high school baseball championship in 1956 and 1960. The 1960 victory marks the last time a school in the city of St. Louis won a state high school championship in the sport.

Beaumont was the first high school in St. Louis to integrate, in 1954. The comprehensive high school was closed in 2014 due to declining enrollment and poor student performance. A small portion of the massive building, still owned by the St. Louis Public School District, houses the Beaumont Technical Center, a two-year technical program for juniors and seniors.

STAN MUSIAL AND BIGGIE'S

6435 Chippewa Street

In 1948, Stan Musial became a full-time citizen of St. Louis after buying his first home on Childress Avenue. Soon after, he built his presence in the St. Louis business community. Baseball players did not earn money like they do today, and Musial was looking for ways to invest so he would have earnings after his baseball career.

Musial met local restaurateur Biggie Garagnani through Cardinals owner Sam Breadon. After seeing Garagnani's restaurant in his new neighborhood, he decided he would like to get in the restaurant business. Biggie was happy to comply. There is no better publicity then having the best player in the National League endorse your restaurant in a baseball-crazy town like St. Louis. Biggie did not ask Musial for a cash investment in the partnership. They made a deal in which Musial's stake in the business ($25,000) would come from future profits.

Early in 1949, Garagnani's restaurant on Chippewa was renamed Stan Musial and Biggie's. Business immediately increased, and the partners profited. After the first year, the restaurant dining room was doubled in size and a cocktail lounge was added. Musial noted in an interview some years later that the revenue went up by $100,000 each year for several years. Their steakhouse became a go-to place in St. Louis.

Musial was involved in the business, not just a celebrity owner. In the off-season, he frequented the restaurant, visited tables and signed autographs. He wanted to make sure the customers had a good experience and personally investigated complaints. He took particular interest in the cuts of meat, making sure the quality served to the customers was high.

Stan Musial and Biggie's on Chippewa Street. *Missouri Historical Society.*

Stan Musial and Biggie's menu, mid-1950s. *Harley Hammerman/Lost Tables.*

Stan Musial and Biggie's on Oakland Avenue. *Missouri Historical Society.*

By 1954, the pair had stakes in four restaurants around town. In 1956, the restaurant dining room was expanded again. In 1961, the old location closed and the pair opened a new Stan Musial and Biggie's at 5130 Oakland Avenue. This location, visible from Highway 40, did very well in the 1960s, hosting many events in the new private dining spaces, including most St. Louis Cardinal team events. The fifty-three-year-old Garagnani unexpectedly died of a heart attack in 1967. Biggie's son continued operating the restaurant, but without Biggie's drive and with Stan backing away from day-to-day operations, business declined. The Oakland Avenue location closed after New Year's Eve, 1986.

Neither building stands. The original location on Chippewa is now occupied by a medical clinic. The St. Louis Science Center occupies the Oakland Avenue location.

Chase Park Plaza Hotel

212 North Kingshighway Boulevard

The original building on this site was designed by architect Preston Bradshaw and erected in 1922 by developer Chase Ullman, who named it the Chase Hotel. It was the most luxurious hotel in the city. Visiting baseball teams stayed at the hotel, as it was less than a mile from Sportsman's Park. It also hosted celebrity performers and Wrestling at the Chase, a popular event featuring pro wrestlers.

With baseball players staying, hijinks were sure to follow. The stories of hotel pranks are uncountable, but one event not directly involving an active player stands out. In 1957, the Pittsburgh Pirate announcer Bob Prince was staying in a third-floor room overlooking the hotel pool. There are different stories about how the event was initiated, but after a wager or a dare with a Pirate ballplayer, a clothed and sober Prince jumped from his hotel balcony into the swimming

Bob Prince. *Society for American Baseball Research.*

pool. While one newspaper claimed that the jump was ninety feet, based on the hotel configuration, it was about twenty-five feet down and several feet out from a third-story room, an impressive jump but not particularly risky for a guy who had a diving background in his younger days.

A more serious event occurred in front of the Chase on November 3, 1968. On a rainy Sunday evening, Cardinal broadcaster Harry Caray tried to cross Kingshighway. He was struck by a car driven by Michael Poliquin. At the time, Caray had been broadcasting Cardinal games for more than twenty years. The popular Caray was well known as a great Budweiser beer salesman and a frequent consumer of the product. News reports at the time did not suggest he was intoxicated when the accident happened.

Caray was seriously injured, suffering compound fractures in each leg, a dislocated shoulder and cuts and bruises. The St. Louis Police, not missing a chance to raise money for the city coffers, issued him a citation for crossing the street outside of a crosswalk and cited Poliquin for not having a driver's license available.

Caray recovered to broadcast games during the 1969 season. The accident led to his departure from the Cardinal broadcasts. August Busch III's wife, Susan, was identified as a frequent caller to Caray's hospital room. In response to this suspected affair with his daughter-in-law, Cardinal owner August Busch II declined to renew Caray's contract after the 1969 season.

The Chase was closed from 1989 until 1999. The Kingsdale partnership financed a $35 million renovation and reopened the building in 2001. After the renovation, Cardinal manager Tony LaRussa was a tenant during the baseball season. Today, the Chase Park Plaza complex,

Left: Chase Park Plaza in the 1930s. *Missouri Historical Society*.

Below: Chase Park Plaza today. *Kathryn Flaspohler*.

consisting of the original historic hotel, a tall art deco tower built in 1927, event spaces, restaurants and bars, remains a sought-after destination. The complex, located in the thriving Central West End neighborhood, is in the National Trust for Historic Preservation's Historic Hotels of America program.

Bow Wow Becomes an Undertaker

14960 Manchester Road

A Bowman Hank Arft baseball card from 1951. *Bowman Gum Company.*

Henry Arft was born in Manchester, Missouri, in 1922, the fifth of six children, on the family farm. When he turned eighteen, the St. Louis Browns signed him to a contract and started him off in the lowest level of the minor leagues. A first baseman, Hank progressed through the Browns' system, but World War II intervened. He enlisted in the U.S. Navy and served three years before returning to the Browns.

St. Louis promoted him to the major league club at the end of July 1948. Arft reached base safely in each of his first 23 games, batting .361. The fans chanting "Arft, Arft, Arft" led to his nickname, "Bow Wow." Like many prospects, he cooled off and never was able to heat back up. His career lasted parts of five seasons, 300 major league games. He hit .253 with 13 home runs. But 2 of those homers were off two Hall of Fame Bobs, Feller and Lemon.

Arft's career included two memorable games a few days apart. On August 19, 1951, he played in the game in which three-foot, seven-inch Eddie Gaedel pinch-hit to lead off the game, drew a walk and prompted a major league rule change. On August 24, Arft was in the lineup for Grandstand Manager Night. Fans in the crowd were given placards and voted on strategy decisions during the game. Hank got a hit driving in two runs during the win, but the fans voted for the less-than-swift player to steal, and he was thrown out.

Arft had something to fall back on after his retirement from baseball. He married Ruth Schrader in 1949, the great-granddaughter of George Schrader, who founded a funeral business in 1868. The funeral home was well established by the time Arft joined the staff, but he settled into the business and remained involved for over fifty years, until he died in 2002. Whenever someone brought up his baseball career or, better yet, called him "Bow Wow," Arft would break into a big, appreciative grin.

Schrader Funeral Home remains in operation today and is the largest family-owned funeral home in the St. Louis area. The fifth generation of the family, Hank's daughter Peggy, and her cousin Steven Schrader, run

Schrader Funeral Home. *Kathryn Flaspohler.*

the business on busy Manchester Road. The large funeral home has stood in the same location since 1910 and expanded several times to meet the needs of the area population, which has grown thirtyfold since 1868. The company provides traditional funeral services and operates a crematorium on the premises.

ANHEUSER-BUSCH BREWERY

Twelfth Street and Lynch Street

Eberhard Anheuser immigrated to St. Louis in 1843. Trained as a soap maker, he started what would become the largest soap and candle company in St. Louis. As that business returned profits, he invested in the Bavarian Brewing Company. By 1860, he was the sole owner and renamed the company E. Anheuser & Company.

Adolphus Busch immigrated to St. Louis in 1857, the second youngest of twenty-two children. He became a partner in a brewery supply business and met Anheuser through this operation. Anheuser introduced Busch to his daughter Lily. Romance bloomed, and Busch became Anheuser's son-

Left: Eberhard Anheuser in the 1860s. *Missouri Historical Society*.

Right: Adolphus Busch in 1868. *Missouri Historical Society*.

in-law. After a few years, Anheuser made Busch a partner in the brewery. In 1879, they named the enterprise Anheuser-Busch Brewing Company.

Busch introduced pasteurization and refrigerated transport, the first brewery to use those technologies. Using these innovations, the company became a nationwide concern and one of the largest breweries in America. Its size helped the company weather Prohibition, as did products such as nonalcoholic beer and sales of yeast, malt extract and hops—the items needed for an enterprising person to make their own beer. After Prohibition was repealed, the company delivered a wagon of beer to the White House pulled by what would become its iconic Clydesdale horse team. Adolphus died in 1913 and was interred in one of the most impressive mausoleums in Bellefontaine Cemetery.

By 1934, Adolphus's grandson August Busch II was president of the company. He was strongly supportive of growing his business and enhancing the city. It seems hard to believe today, but the St. Louis Cardinals were in danger of moving to another city in 1952. Cardinal owner Fred Saigh pled guilty to tax evasion and was forced by the league to sell the team. Texas

From left, Adolphus III, August I and August II with the first beer delivered to the White House after Prohibition's repeal. *Missouri Historical Society*.

The Anheuser-Busch Brewery complex. *Kathryn Flaspohler*.

businessmen put up a generous offer, and it looked like the Cardinals would move to Houston. Busch II, using the brewery's money, purchased the team, even though their offer was less than the Texans. Saigh preferred to sell it to St. Louis interests to keep the team in town.

Busch II was a practical sportsman who used the team as a marketing tool to sell beer. He proposed changing the name of Sportsman's Park to Budweiser Stadium, but the league rejected the name as too commercial. Instead, he settled on Busch Memorial Stadium, after his father. Two years later, the company introduced Busch Beer. So Gussie, as he was fondly referred to, got a stadium named after one of the company's products. By 1957, Anheuser-Busch was the largest brewery in the United States and would continue to grow and outpace the competition.

Gussie Busch died in 1989 at the age of ninety. The brewery sold the team to William DeWitt II in 1996. In 2008, Anheuser-Busch Brewery merged with In-Bev to become the world's largest brewery. The St. Louis plant, a National Historic Landmark, remains in operation today. Free tours of the brewing operation, including the historic brewhouse and a visit with Clydesdale horses in the carriage house, make this a popular destination with locals and tourists.

Youngster Witnesses Hero's Record

4459 Clarence Avenue

On May 2, 1954, Nate Colbert Sr. collected his eight-year-old son, and the pair took the streetcar to Sportsman's Park to watch the St. Louis Cardinals. A Sunday doubleheader was scheduled—two games for the price of one was always a good idea for the former semipro baseball player. The opponent that day was the New York Giants, led by the transcendent Willie Mays.

Nate Jr.'s favorite player was not Mays. He was a Cardinal fan, and his hero was Stan Musial. In the first inning, Musial drew a walk against Giants ace Johnny Antonelli. In the third inning, Stan cracked a solo home run. In the fifth inning, he hit a two-run shot off Antonelli. In the eighth, with the game tied, 6–6, Musial came up against reliever Jim Hearn. He homered for the third time, this one a three-run shot that gave the Cardinals a 9–6 lead. They won the game, 10–6.

Both Nates were thrilled with Musial's performance: 3 home runs and 6 RBIs in the game and a Cardinal win. There was no way Musial would sit

Left: Nate Colbert after his record day. *National Baseball Hall of Fame and Museum.*

Right: Colbert's childhood home. *Kathryn Flaspohler.*

out game two. He was in the middle of a streak of 895 consecutive games played, still the eighth-longest streak in major league history. There was more slugging in this game. In the first inning, Stan walked. In the third, he flew out to Mays, his first out of the day. In the fifth, the Cardinals were trailing, 8–3, when "The Man" homered again, a two-run shot. In the seventh, he hit a solo shot, his fifth home run of the day, cutting the lead to 8–7. He had one last chance in the bottom of the ninth but popped out. The Giants won the game, 9–7.

It was a record-setting performance. Musial was the first major leaguer to hit five home runs in a single day and the first to hit five home runs over two consecutive games. The Colberts marveled about Musial all the way home.

Years later, Nate Jr. was the star of Sumner High School's baseball team. The hometown Cardinals signed him in 1964. A year later, the Houston Astros selected him in the Rule 5 draft. Two years later, San Diego selected him in the 1968 expansion draft. Nate became the Padres' first power hitter, putting up five excellent seasons for them. In 1972, he had his best year, hitting 38 home runs and finishing eighth in the Most Valuable Player voting.

On August 1, 1972, the Padres were in Atlanta for a doubleheader. Colbert had an achy knee but wanted to be in the lineup to take advantage of that home-run-friendly park. In the first game, he went 4 for 5 with 2 home runs and 5 runs batted in in the 9–0 win. With a chronically bad back, which eventually forced his early retirement, he would normally not play the second game of a doubleheader. But after the first game, he asked to be placed into the lineup. During game two, he hit 3 home runs and drove in 8 in another Padre win, 11–7.

Colbert matched his hero's record of five home runs in a doubleheader. He set new doubleheader records with 13 RBIs and 22 total bases, both still standing.

Colbert's childhood home on Clarence Avenue, built in 1912, has been divided into two units and remains residential property.

That Guy Really Delivers the Milk

4071 Keokuk Street

Most professional ballplayers are remarkably anonymous. There have been more than twenty thousand major league players, and about 25 percent of them appeared in the big leagues in a single season. Another 25 percent appeared in fewer than five seasons. It seems a glamorous job, but the majority of people who appeared in uniform had their moment of fame and then went on with their lives.

Bill Jennings is a St. Louis example of one of these players. He was born in

Bill Jennings in 1951. *St. Louis Browns.*

St. Louis in 1925 and attended Southwest High School, where he was a star on the baseball and basketball teams. He enlisted in the U.S. Navy in 1944, serving as a radioman on the fast-attack transport USS *Gosper*. After his military service, the New York Giants signed him. He toiled in the minor leagues for six seasons before the St. Louis Browns picked him up halfway through the 1951 season.

Jennings's half season with the Browns was eventful. The team was bad, winning 52 and losing 102 while finishing last in the American League. Owner Bill Veeck did what he could to draw fans. Jennings was in the lineup when the dwarf Eddie Gaedel pinch-hit, drawing a walk and creating a publicity stir that forced the league

Grbic Restaurant. *Kathryn Flaspohler.*

to change its rules when Veeck threatened to lead him off every game. Jennings hit a meager .179 in his half season and found himself back in the minor leagues.

Bill played two more seasons in the minors before giving up baseball and moving back to St. Louis. He had a family to support, and a minor league baseball salary was not up to the task. He went to work as a deliveryman for Bailey Farm Dairy in south St. Louis. He worked for the dairy for thirty-five years, raised three daughters and was a solid member of the community. He attended baseball events for many years and was always a humble and engaging individual. He died in 2010 and is interred in Jefferson Barracks National Cemetery.

Bailey Farm Dairy closed in the early 1990s. The complex on Keokuk Street was purchased in 1998 by Suljman Grbic as a surprise anniversary gift for his wife, Erbina. The couple turned it into a restaurant and event space. They and their children continue to run the business. The Bosnian-themed Grbic Restaurant has been named the best Bosnian restaurant in St. Louis several times by the *Riverfront Times*. The Grbic family embraces the Bailey Farm legacy, displaying the original sign inside the restaurant and keeping a selection of Bailey Farm memorabilia.

THE REDHEAD

9101 South Broadway

Nicknames are part of baseball. There are many clever ones and many that require no explanation at all. Albert Schoendienst had one of the latter. One look at his ginger head, and a singular nickname made sense: "Red."

Schoendienst was signed by the St. Louis Cardinals as an amateur free agent before the 1942 season. He toiled in the minor leagues and served a year in the military before finding his way to the big leagues in 1945. He was the starting second baseman on the World Series–winning 1946 team and played in nine All-Star Games while occupying second for the Cardinals. During the 1956 season, the noncompetitive Cardinals traded Schoendienst to the New York Giants for Alvin Dark in a ten-player trade.

Albert "Red" Schoendienst's 1948 rookie baseball card. *Bowman Gum Company.*

Schoendienst, from Germantown, Illinois, was shocked by the trade. He had made St. Louis his home. He lived on Potomac Street in the early 1950s and moved a few blocks south in the mid-1950s to live near his lifelong friend Stan Musial. His family, also surprised by the trade, stayed in St. Louis while he rented a place in New York. The following season, he was traded to the Milwaukee Braves. The family rented a home there during the season and returned to St. Louis during the off-season.

In 1958, still with the Braves, Schoendienst had no energy and worried about his health. He was diagnosed with tuberculosis and checked in to Mount St. Rose Hospital on South Broadway, just outside St. Louis's city limits. The hospital was the first tuberculosis sanitarium west of the Mississippi when it was established in 1901. The doctors removed part of Red's lung to speed recovery. Baseball fans nationwide, including President Dwight Eisenhower, sent more than ten thousand pieces of mail wishing him a speedy recovery.

The treatment worked. Red returned to play for the Braves in 1960, then came back to St. Louis for two seasons as a pinch-hitter and backup second baseman. At that point, he was hired as a coach. In 1964, his first full year as coach, the team won the World Series. In a surprise move, Johnny Keane resigned as manager. The team selected Schoendienst to manage. He led the team for twelve seasons, winning two pennants and the World Series in 1967. He was fired after the team finished fifth in 1976 and left to coach for the Oakland A's. Two years later, he was back in the St. Louis dugout as hitting coach, and he would not leave again.

Schoendienst stepped up to manage partial seasons twice more when the Cardinals were in transition between managers. He stayed in uniform for most games until 2011, when the eighty-eight-year-old decided

Mount St. Rose Sanitarium in the 1950s. *Jesuit Online Library*.

Schoendienst home on Potomac. *Kathryn Flaspohler*.

he could not hit fungoes like he used to. Schoendienst passed away in 2018 at the age of ninety-five. He is buried in Resurrection Cemetery on MacKenzie Road.

The hospital, run by the Sisters of St. Mary, closed in 1984. The main hospital building was torn down in 1988, and a new building was constructed for Hancock Place Elementary School. The convent building was converted into a preschool, and a single-story building, added to the hospital complex in 1980, was retained for school use. Schoendienst's home on Potomac Street remains a single-family residence.

Jack Buck Is Fired

5405 Elizabeth Avenue

It seems inconceivable that Jack Buck, the most beloved broadcaster in St. Louis Cardinal history, was fired by the team early in his broadcast career. The firing left him in a spot, as he had a wife and six kids to feed.

Buck began his broadcasting career in Columbus, Ohio. After his military service in World War II, including receiving a Purple Heart, he attended The Ohio State University. He worked for WCOL in Columbus, and his first baseball play-by-play job was broadcasting the Columbus Redbirds, the Cardinals' AAA team. He did other sports and news broadcasting, getting a breadth of experience.

In 1952, WCOL quit broadcasting Redbird games, and Buck was fired. He did television work but felt he was better suited for radio. In 1953, he took a job broadcasting the Rochester Red Wings, another Cardinal minor league affiliate. He auditioned for the Cardinals' major league broadcasts and got the job for the 1954 season.

Buck joined a broadcast team consisting of Harry Caray and Milo Hamilton. Caray was the dominant personality in the booth, doing most innings. He always wanted to be on the microphone when something great happened. After one season, Hamilton left and Joe Garagiola was hired. Caray liked Garagiola, and the chemistry between Buck and Caray was not good. Jack was slowly phased out of the booth. He did not travel to away games and did commercials and other sports for the station.

Buck felt secure enough to buy a house in 1955 on Elizabeth Avenue for his burgeoning family. They stayed until 1959, when he sought a new house in Ladue, needing more room for his large family. After he purchased

From left, Jack Buck,
Harry Caray and
Joe Garagiola.
KMOX Radio.

Jack Buck's home on Elizabeth Avenue. *Brian Flaspohler.*

the new home, the Cardinals hired Buddy Blattner to be Caray's broadcast partner and fired Buck. He found out right before Christmas.

KMOX general manager Robert Hyland did not want someone of Buck's talent to broadcast elsewhere. He hired Buck to host the news and talk show *At Your Service* and gave him the freedom to do other sports, including baseball and football nationally. Hyland insisted that the Cardinals would be back for Jack. Two years later, the team hired Buck to broadcast again. He and Caray had a much better relationship the second time around, and the rest is history.

Buck's home on Elizabeth Avenue, a handsome red-brick, two-story structure, is the larger of the two in the duplex. This block of Elizabeth is called Hall of Fame Way to honor Buck as well as Yogi Berra and Joe Garagiola, whose childhood homes are nearby.

Red Bird Bowling Lanes

7339 Gravois Road

St. Louis was a bowling mecca in the 1950s and 1960s. Two former teammates, Stan Musial and Joe Garagiola, invested in this phenomenon when they bought into Red Bird Bowling Lanes, a South City bowling alley. They each owned a third of the business; the remaining third was owned by Biggie Garagnani, Musial's restaurant partner.

The full-service bowling paradise, with thirty-two lanes, a snack bar, a cocktail lounge, a nursery and meeting rooms, was open twenty-four hours. It was a popular and profitable business for many years, and the partners thrived. Unfortunately, business partnerships do not always work out. In 1985, Garagiola sued the other two partners over payments to Musial's son and Garagnani's son for services the lawsuit claimed were never performed. The suit also claimed that the bowling alley business loaned money to Musial and Garagnani's restaurant.

This seems to be the only time anyone has said anything negative about Musial on the record. Garagiola, in a moment of anger, said, "Stan is not a nice man." Musial was deeply hurt by the lawsuit and the comment. The lawsuit was settled for an undisclosed amount, and the business was sold by the partners in 1986.

Sadly, former teammates Musial and Garagiola never reconciled. Joe tried to mend fences in the 1990s, but Musial rejected every overture. Jack

Left: Newspaper ad for the new Red Bird Lanes bowling alley. St. Louis Post-Dispatch.

Below: Stan Musial, Joe Garagiola and Yogi Berra during happy times. *National Baseball Hall of Fame and Museum*.

Buck would sometimes tease Musial by asking if he ever heard from Joe. Musial, knowing what was coming, would say, "DiMaggio?" Then Buck would emphasize, "Garagiola!" During the 2006 World Series, Musial was scheduled to throw out the first pitch before game three. He found out that Garagiola was going to catch it, so he called in sick. After Garagiola returned home to Arizona, Stan, now fully recovered, threw out the first pitch before game five.

The dated bowling alley continued under new ownership but was closed in 1996 and torn down for redevelopment. A Walgreens drugstore occupies the site.

KEANE QUITS

8816a St. Charles Rock Road

St. Louis native son Johnny Keane lived with his parents on St. Charles Rock Road, in a home above a vacant storefront. The St. Louis Cardinals were impressed with the nineteen-year-old's play in the amateur leagues in town and signed him in 1930 as a shortstop.

Keane played in the minor leagues for thirteen years, advancing as high as the AA team in Rochester, Illinois, but a contact-hitting shortstop with

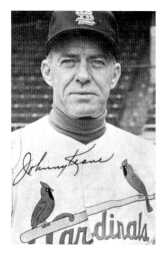

A Johnny Keane signed five-by-seven-inch photo. *Heritage Auctions.*

little power didn't impress St. Louis brass. Instead, they appreciated his keen knowledge of the game and ability to lead people, so they installed him as manager—and player—for their D League team in Albany, Georgia, in 1938. Keane proved successful as manager and advanced through the Cardinal system.

After thirty-one years with the Cardinals, Keane finally got his chance to manage at the major league level. Solly Hemus, whose bias against African American players was evident, led an underperforming team. He was fired midway through the 1961 season, and the team promoted Keane to manage. He let Bob Gibson know he would get a start every fifth day and told Curt Flood he was the everyday regular in center. Keane rebuilt the clubhouse culture, which was in tatters under Hemus.

Keane's childhood home (*second story*) today. *Kathryn Flaspohler.*

The young Cardinals responded. In 1962, the team was above .500 but finished sixth in a ten-team league. In 1963, they jumped into second place, 6 games behind the Los Angeles Dodgers. With high expectations, they started the 1964 season slowly. After a loss on July 24, the team was 47-48, 10 games behind Philadelphia. Keane heard through the grapevine that he would be fired, so he prepared his letter of resignation. The midseason acquisition of a young Lou Brock from the Chicago Cubs sparked the team. They played very well in the second half to finish 93-69, a game ahead of Philadelphia and Cincinnati. The team won the World Series against the New York Yankees.

Cardinals owner August Busch II held a postseason news conference to announce Keane's retention for the 1965 season. Nevertheless, the proud Keane had made up his mind to leave. He negotiated a backroom deal to replace New York Yankee manager Yogi Berra. Before the news conference, he gave Mr. Busch his resignation letter. An unprepared Busch held an awkward meeting with the press, announcing Keane's departure.

Keane managed the Yankees for one full season. Three weeks into his second season, he was fired after the team started 4-16. He returned to

Houston to begin an enforced retirement. One year later, the fifty-five-year-old died of a heart attack.

Keane's childhood home on St. Charles Rock Road is still a second-floor single-family apartment. A sports bar now occupies the first floor.

A Palace For Cardinals and Cardinals

250 Stadium Plaza

As soon as August Busch II bought the St. Louis Cardinals in 1953, he started lobbying for a new downtown stadium for his team. Sportsman's Park, last renovated in 1908, was showing its age, and Gussie wanted a new stadium he could use to maximize revenue. A few years later, the city enticed a National Football League team, the Chicago Cardinals, to move to St. Louis, in part with the promise of a new stadium.

Why not kill two birds with one stone? In the 1950s and 1960s, several multipurpose stadiums were built for baseball and football teams. In Washington, D.C., the first modern multipurpose stadium was constructed, and several more followed. St. Louis proposed a downtown stadium that would revitalize a decaying area of the city, including St. Louis's small Chinatown district. The district, associated with Chinese immigrants since 1869, housed restaurants, laundries, groceries, tea shops and opium dens. It was removed by eminent domain.

The new stadium was designed by Sverdrup & Parcel. Edward Durell Stone designed the arched roof, meant to evoke the Gateway Arch, completed in 1965. Ground-breaking took place on May 25, 1964, and the stadium was completed on May 12, 1966. Costs were estimated at $24 million ($191 million in 2021 dollars). Financing was primarily covered by the city, with the baseball and football teams contributing $5 million each. Anheuser-Busch bought the stadium from the city for $51 million in 1981.

As part of the pregame ceremonies on the stadium's opening day, home plate was flown by helicopter from Sportsman's Park. The helicopter landed in the outfield and discharged its precious cargo, which was installed on the field.

The stadium was well received by fans. A modern facility was appreciated after all the years of Sportsman's Park. The park opened with a grass field, but Astroturf was installed in 1970 because it could handle the damage from both baseball and football teams and the hot St. Louis summers. Even before the turf, the stadium was recognized as a hot place to play. Yankee manager

Aerial view of Busch Memorial Stadium during the 1982 World Series. *State Historical Society of Missouri.*

Casey Stengal, at the 1966 All-Star Game, remarked, "The new park sure holds the heat well. It took the press right out of my pants."

The football Cardinals left for Arizona after the 1987 season, but the turf remained until significant stadium renovations in 1996. Many upperdeck seats in the outfield were removed and replaced with a hand-operated scoreboard, grass was reinstalled on the field, championship flags and retired number flags were installed and other changes were made to mark the venue as the Cardinals' sole domain.

The park hosted six World Series during its lifetime, with St. Louis winning in 1967 and 1982. Mark McGwire set the home record in 1998

Busch Memorial Stadium infield marked on the Ballpark Village plaza. *Brian Flaspohler.*

(since eclipsed). His record-setting 62nd home run and his 70th of the season were hit in the park. After the 2005 season, the park was demolished to make room for the new Busch Stadium, the current home of the St. Louis Cardinals. The site of the former stadium is now occupied by Ballpark Village, a complex of restaurants, bars, shops and the Cardinals Hall of Fame and Museum. The approximate location of the old infield is marked in the Ballpark Village plaza.

Gibson Has a Year

6316 Westminster Place

Bob Gibson, the greatest pitcher in St. Louis Cardinals' franchise history, maintained his permanent residence in his hometown of Omaha, Nebraska. Each year, he rented a place in St. Louis for the baseball season. In 1968, he rented a home on Westminster Place. Based on his results in 1968, he probably wanted to rent the same home for 1969.

After Gibson's first three starts—two seven-inning outings and a complete game—he had a great 2.35 ERA but only one decision, a loss suffered to the Chicago Cubs. In his next seven starts, he allowed a total of 9 earned runs, but due to the Cardinal offense providing lackluster run support, his record was 3-5, with a low 1.52 ERA.

A publicity photo of Bob Gibson and Clint Howard promoting Gibson's 1968 guest appearance on the show *Gentle Ben. CBS.*

On June 2, "Hoot" (after Western movie star Hoot Gibson) began an unprecedented pitching streak. He had 12 starts in June and July, winning and completing all 12 games. He threw 8 shutouts, including a streak of 47 scoreless innings. His record stood at 15-5, and his ERA was 0.96.

In August and September, he was still brilliant although not quite at the June/July level. His final numbers on the season were a 22-9 record with a 1.12 ERA. He completed 28 of his 34 starts, threw 13 shutouts and led the league with 268 strikeouts. He won the Cy Young and the Most Valuable Player Awards and a Rawlings Gold Glove. The Cardinals won the National League pennant by nine games over the San Francisco Giants but were trimmed in the World Series, four games to three, by the Detroit Tigers. Bob's 1.12 ERA was the lowest of any pitcher throwing over 200 innings since Dutch Leonard's 0.96 ERA in 1914 and has not been bested since.

Gibson was a fierce competitor with a wicked slider who won 251 games for the Cardinals over his career. One of his famous characteristics was his complete nonfraternization with anyone not wearing a Cardinal uniform. Even during All-Star Games, he would ignore his teammates from other NL teams. He cultivated a reputation as an intimidating presence on the mound by his mannerisms and his explosive delivery to home plate. Teammates and competitors frequently named him as the most competitive player in the game.

Gibson stayed in the Cardinal organization his entire playing career, a rare achievement. The team retired his number 45 as soon as he stepped away in 1975. In 1981, he was inducted into the Baseball Hall of Fame. After he retired, he coached for a few seasons and returned to St. Louis for baseball events and reunions, including Cardinals Hall of Fame gatherings

Gibson's rental today. *Brian Flaspohler.*

and the opening day parade of Cardinal heroes. As he mellowed over the years, his sense of humor revealed itself at times, particularly with his old friends and teammates. Gibson passed away from pancreatic cancer in 2020.

The large brick home Bob rented, built in 1920, remains a private dwelling.

An Artist on the Field and Off

8007 Clayton Road

Curt Flood was a defensive wizard with a solid bat who covered centerfield for the St. Louis Cardinals throughout the 1960s. He came up through the Cincinnati Reds organization, briefly making the majors before being traded to St. Louis in December 1957. Once in St. Louis under the watchful eye of Johnny Keane, Flood blossomed into a good hitter to go with his masterful skills in the field.

Flood was an excellent painter. He opened his own portrait studio in Clayton, where he painted as a way to relieve the stress of playing baseball

Lou Brock (*left*) and Bob Gibson (*center*) portraits painted by Curt Flood (*right*). *Artranked.com*.

and of life. His turbulent marriage ended in a 1966 divorce, and he worried about taking care of his five children financially. While he was paid well relative to a middle-class wage earner, baseball players did not earn the large sums available in the game today, and Flood knew his playing career was limited. His portrait studio was one of many business interests he invested in.

Flood did a number of well-received portraits. His goal was to make faithful reproductions from the pictures he was given. At one point, he told a *St. Louis Post-Dispatch* reporter that he had a backlog of commissions for over fifty paintings and would have more if he had more time to paint.

In 1969, Flood held out, requesting a $100,000 salary from the Cardinals. (He had been paid $72,500 the previous year.) They came to terms at $90,000, but August Busch II did not appreciate players who fought management. Flood had a good season in 1969, but the Cardinals traded him to the Philadelphia Phillies in the off-season.

Flood refused to report. He did not want to leave St. Louis, at least without some say into where he might go. Using the Major League Baseball Players Association lawyers, he sued Major League Baseball, ultimately losing his case. Although he lost, he is considered one of the pioneers for players receiving free agency because of the high-profile case.

In 1970, while his case was in the courts, instead of staying in shape, he spent too much time, in his words, "bedding and boozing." To make matters worse, his businesses in St. Louis failed due to his fading involvement. In 1971, he accepted a trade to the Washington Senators. He reported but was in no condition to play. After thirteen poor games, he was released. His baseball career was over.

Flood's portrait studio today. *Kathryn Flaspohler.*

Flood struggled with sobriety and finances after his baseball career. He spent some time in Spain and in Los Angeles, freeing himself from drink in the early 1990s. In 1995, he was diagnosed with throat cancer and died from the disease in 1997.

The Colonial-style building with a Greek-inspired façade where Flood did his portrait painting is used today by a promotional products company.

1975–PRESENT

THIS IS NOT YOUR FANTASY FOOTBALL PLAQUE

15472 Manchester Road

In the fall of 1985, UPS driver Carl Riechers stopped by All-Star Awards for the morning delivery. He walked into the business and was stunned to see eighteen Gold Glove Awards ready for packaging and shipping. Being a baseball fan, he stopped to see who was receiving awards, a month before the official announcement would be made.

As Carl scanned the shiny trophies, many of the names were not a surprise: Ozzie Smith, Keith Hernandez, Willie McGee, George Brett, Dwight Evans, Tony Pena. But he saw one name that gave him pause. Ron Quidry was listed on the American League pitcher Gold Glove Award plaque. Ron Quidry? He never heard of him. Riechers pointed out the oddity to one of the company representatives, who whisked the trophy away. The award was supposed to go to Ron Guidry, but poor legibility led to an engraving error.

When Carl returned for pickups that evening, the award had been corrected by All-Star Awards personnel. That was a good thing, because some pipefitter in New York named Ron Quidry would have been surprised when the AL Gold Glove showed up at his house!

All-Star Awards, a St. Louis company, supplied Rawlings with the Gold Glove Awards in the 1980s and 1990s. The company was purchased by

Left: Ron Quidry's Gold Glove Award? *Brian Flaspohler.*

Below: All-Star Trophy's location for over thirty years, now shuttered. *Kathryn Flaspohler.*

Collegiate Awards in 2020, and its showroom moved four miles east. The showroom on Manchester where Ron Quidry's award was handled now sits vacant. Collegiate Awards is the Midwest's premier source for quality awards and recognition items. It supplies awards and trophies for any occasion, including corporate recognition items, softball league trophies and fantasy football plaques. And it still counts Rawlings Sporting Goods as a customer.

THE MOON MAN SERVES MEALS

620 Market Street

Mike Shannon has been in the radio booth so long, most fans today have no idea of his playing career. He celebrated his fiftieth year in the booth in 2021 and retired at the end of the season. He was never as crisp or professional as his longtime partner, Jack Buck, but he endeared himself to St. Louis Cardinal fans with his enthusiasm and his evocative—and at times inexplicable—game descriptions.

Shannon was born in St. Louis in 1939. He attended Christian Brothers College High School and was a three-sport star, in baseball, football and basketball. Many colleges offered scholarships to the young quarterback, who was being touted as a future Heisman winner, but when the St. Louis Cardinals came calling with a contract and $50,000, Shannon went to baseball. Years later, he said he was better at football but liked playing baseball more and the money made his decision for him.

Shannon had a nice playing career for the Cardinals. He was an outfielder, playing right field in the first half of his career. In 1967, the Cardinals traded for Roger Maris, and the team asked Shannon to move to third base. He worked hard at the transition and ended up an okay fielder at the hot corner, particularly in 1968. His teammates called him "Moon Man" for a play in which he moved oddly to avoid being hit by a pitch and because of the way he moved between subjects during conversations, leaving the listener confounded. Shannon stayed busy in his off-seasons, raising six kids with his high school sweetheart, Judy.

Shannon's career highlights include a game-tying home run in the 1964 World Series and roles on both Cardinal World Series championship teams in 1964 and 1967. But in 1970, he was diagnosed with a life-threatening kidney disease. He underwent treatment and attempted a comeback. Doctors intervened, and his playing career was over. He spent a year in the team's marketing department and then was paired with Jack Buck for the radio broadcasts.

No one who heard those first few seasons would have thought Shannon would last fifty years in the booth. Buck proved to be a good teacher and mentor to the raw broadcaster. Shannon would never be a great play-by-play guy, but he endeared himself to the Cardinal fan base. Signature calls like, "Get up, baby, get up!" on a Cardinal home run, along with wacky descriptions were common. A personal favorite was when a fast player

Mike Shannon horsing around in a celebrity baseball game, 1968. *State Historical Society of Missouri.*

Mike Shannon's Steaks and Seafood's downtown location. *Kathryn Flaspohler.*

went from first to third. Shannon would exclaim, "That guy can really deliver the mail!"

In 1986, already a fixture in the community, Shannon opened Mike Shannon's Steaks and Seafood restaurant on Market Street in downtown St. Louis. With a private room in the basement filled with classic photos of ballplayers and plenty of memorabilia in the main dining room, the upscale eatery attracted people for thirty years before closing in 2016 under competitive pressure from the new Ballpark Village venues. Shannon still owns two Mike Shannon's Grill locations, in Edwardsville, Illinois, and at St. Louis's Lambert Airport.

Shannon retired from broadcasting after the 2021 season. The downtown restaurant location is unoccupied.

THE WIZARD'S SPORTS BAR

645 West Port Plaza Drive

Ozzie Smith in 1983. *John Max Mena.*

There can be only one greatest fielder at any particular position. The majority of fans, even today, would not argue with the claim that Ozzie Smith was baseball's greatest defender at shortstop.

The Southern California native had played four seasons for the San Diego Padres when Whitey Herzog traded Garry Templeton for him after the 1981 season. He was already recognized as a wizard in the field, but his career batting average was a paltry .231 with no power. Herzog was not worried about the offense; he wanted the glove.

Ozzie played fifteen seasons with St. Louis. His offense improved, and his career batting average for the Redbirds was .272. While he did not hit many home runs, he did club a memorable one in the 1985 playoffs against the Los Angeles Dodgers, leading to one of Jack Buck's most famous calls: "Go crazy, folks, go crazy!"

Smith fielded the position like no one else. Flashy, with great range, he made all the plays. He had an average throwing arm but made up for it by getting rid of the ball faster than anyone. Later in his career, he suffered

Kobe Restaurant in Westport Plaza. *Brian Flaspohler.*

from shoulder injuries and his arm was weaker, but it never seemed to matter. He always got the ball to first just in time, saving his rare hard throw for the fast runners.

Smith was also known for his signature on-field backflip. On opening day, he would head out to his position and flip. He debuted this move with the Padres on the last game of the 1978 season. Teammate Gene Tenace saw him flipping during spring training and suggested he do a flip before a game, when his daughters could see it. Ozzie found out that Tenace's daughters were at the game, and he flipped as he went to his position. Cardinal fans also embraced the show and went wild when he performed the backflip. Being part of World Series teams in 1982, 1985 and 1987, winning in 1982 and making St. Louis his home endeared him even more to fans.

Preparing for a post-baseball career, "The Wizard" opened an eatery in Westport Plaza, Ozzie's Restaurant and Sports Bar. Determined to enter the business right, Smith teamed up with experienced restaurateurs Ray Gallardo and Patrick Hanon. Opened in 1989, the restaurant featured a multitude of flat-screen TVs, servers in team uniforms and sports memorabilia. The menu was more upscale than a typical sports bar, and Ozzie often mingled with guests before having his own dinner there.

After thirty years in business, the restaurant closed in 2009, shortly after Albert Pujols' restaurant opened in Westport Plaza. The owners believed there was not enough business for two sports-themed restaurants in the complex. A downtown location, which Smith lent his name to but did not own, opened on Washington Avenue in 2010. It lasted a little more than a year before closing. Now, an Ozzie's Burger Bar operates inside Lumiere Place Hotel and Casino. The original location of Ozzie's restaurant at Westport Plaza is now occupied by Kobe, a Japanese steakhouse.

THE COUNTY GETS IN ON THE ACTION

17050 Clayton Road

Baseball in the city of St. Louis as a youth sport has been on a long decline. The last high school from the city to win a Missouri State Championship in the sport was the baseball factory of Beaumont High, in 1960. Since then, many suburban schools have won, marking the move of baseball as a youth sport out of the city.

Lafayette High School is the successor to Beaumont High in generating major league ballplayers. The school, which opened in 1960, had its first major league graduate in 1992. Scarborough Green was drafted by the St. Louis Cardinals and made his major league debut in 1997. After a handful of games, he returned to the majors with the Texas Rangers in 1999 and 2000.

The second graduate to make the majors made a big splash. Ryan Howard graduated in 1997. He won the National League Rookie of the Year Award for the Philadelphia Phillies in 2005 and the National League Most Valuable Player Award in 2006. He suffered from injuries later in his career but smashed 382 home runs in his thirteen-year career.

Hometown playoff and World Series hero David Freese is another Lafayette High grad. He provided heroics in both the National League Championship Series and the World Series, leading the Cardinals to the title in 2011. His home run in the eleventh inning of game six, leading to Joe Buck's famous call, "We'll see you tomorrow night!," is one of the most exciting moments in Cardinals history. Freese retired in 2019, having played eleven seasons for the Cardinals, Los Angeles Angels, Pittsburgh Pirates and Los Angeles Dodgers.

New York Yankee first baseman Luke Voit is the lone active major league player from Lafayette as of the 2021 season. Voit broke in with the Cardinals

Clockwise from top left: Scarborough Green, Ryan Howard, Jeff Gray, David Freese, Matt Buschmann, Luke Voit. *Brian Flaspohler/Kathryn Flaspohler/public domain*.

Lafayette High School baseball field. *Kathryn Flaspohler*.

in 2017 and was traded to the Yankees in 2018. He has struggled with injuries but has hit 73 career home runs through the 2021 season.

Matt Buschmann and Jeff Gray round out the Lafayette graduates. Six major leaguers in twenty years is a good record for a school not in the sunbelt or in Latin America.

Lafayette High School's baseball program has won three Missouri State Championships and finished secon d four times. Oddly, all the victories were in the early 1970s, a period when no future major leaguers played at the school and the high school was where Crestwood Middle School is today. The school moved to its present location in 1989, and all the major league alumni graduated from the current location.

The Stars Shine Here

6643 Delmar Boulevard

The St. Louis Walk of Fame is largely the creation of Joe Edwards, the mastermind behind the formation and growth of the Delmar Loop, a six-block stretch between Trinity Avenue and Des Peres Avenue in University City. This street has been named "One of the Ten Great Streets of America" by the American Planning Association. There are over 140 businesses, including restaurants, gift stores, galleries, theaters, boutiques and live-music spaces.

Interspersed on the sidewalk is the St. Louis Walk of Fame, which honors people who are from St. Louis or spent their creative years in the St. Louis area. Each honoree gets a star in the sidewalk and a short biography. Baseball

From left: Dizzy Dean, Babe Ruth and Paul Dean in 1936. *Missouri Historical Society.*

Dizzy Dean's star on Delmar Avenue. *Kathryn Flaspohler.*

luminaries Stan Musial, Lou Brock, Jack Buck, Yogi Berra and Bob Gibson are among those honored.

On May 18, 1997, Jay Hanna "Dizzy" Dean was among the honorees. In the 1930s, there was only one bigger star than Dean in baseball, and his last name was Ruth. The brash, self-promoting farmboy who could fog the high hard one to batters was hugely popular for his talents and his personification of the country bumpkin playing ball.

Dean's Cardinal debut came during the last game in the 1930 season. He pitched nine innings, allowing only 1 run, but the team was afraid his antics would be more trouble than he was worth. They sent him back to the minors for the 1931 season to mature. In 1932, he was back in the majors to stay. He won 18 games in 1932 and 20 in 1933. Before the 1934 season, he boasted that he and his younger brother Paul would win 45 games. He underestimated their final total—the pair won 49 games in the regular season and 4 more in the World Series. Dizzy won 30 that season, the last National League pitcher to win so many. He led the Cardinals to a World Series victory over Detroit, winning the Most Valuable Player Award.

Dizzy won 134 games for the Gashouse Gang over seven seasons. His career was cut short by returning too quickly from a broken toe suffered in the All-Star Game. His altered pitching delivery caused something in his great right arm to pop. After that, he pitched a few partial seasons with the Chicago Cubs, but the arm was done. He did plenty to impress the Hall of Fame voters, who elected him in 1953.

Dean went on to be a popular broadcaster of Cardinal and Brown games, using his homespun wisdom and poor grammar. "He slud into second," was a normal utterance. He was critical of the Browns during a broadcast in 1947. The team invited him to come out of the broadcast booth and pitch a game for them. The out-of-shape broadcaster who hadn't pitched in six years and whose fastball was long gone threw four scoreless innings and cracked a double, "sludding" into second. After the double, Dean's wife hustled down to the dugout and insisted the manager remove Dizzy from the game before he hurt himself. He proved so popular on his broadcasts that he moved to television and did the national game of the week for several years.

Dean retired with his wife to Mississippi and died in 1974 at the age of sixty-four from a heart attack.

Mad Max

369 North Woods Mill Road

Max Scherzer in 2021. *All-Pro Reels Photography*.

The greatest player from the St. Louis area has long been considered to be Yogi Berra. However, Chesterfield native Max Scherzer is giving Yogi a run for his money. His competitive nature and intensity during games is emphasized by his heterochromia iridum. This condition, in him marked by a blue right eye and a brown left eye, gives Scherzer an especially menacing glare, which he uses when he is not happy with an umpire or when a batter has the nerve to get a big hit.

Scherzer, born in 1984, attended Parkway Central High School in Chesterfield, Missouri, playing baseball, basketball and football. The athlete impressed his hometown Cardinals enough to draft him in the forty-third round of the 2003 baseball draft. Instead of signing for what would have been a small bonus, Scherzer bet on himself

Parkway Central's baseball field. *Kathryn Flaspohler.*

and accepted a baseball scholarship from the University of Missouri. The Tiger coaching staff helped him harness his in-game intensity and cleaned up his pitching mechanics. He responded with a great season in 2005, when he was named Big 12 Pitcher of the Year.

The Arizona Diamondbacks chose Scherzer eleventh overall in the first round of the 2006 draft, 1,280 spots earlier than his draft position in 2003. Diamondbacks staff started calling him "Mad Max" after being exposed to his intensity on the mound. He spent one full season in the Diamondbacks minor league system, making his major league debut on April 29, 2008. He pitched four and one-third perfect innings, setting the major league record for most batters retired in a row at the start of a career. His time in Arizona marked him as a hard thrower with control issues, and the Diamondbacks traded him to the Detroit Tigers in 2009.

In Detroit, Scherzer came into his own. He won 82 games for the team in five seasons and the AL Cy Young Award in 2013. Before the 2014 season, he bet on himself again. Detroit offered a $144 million contract. He declined, determined to play one more season and test the free agent market. He won 18 games in 2014, avoided injury and was rewarded with a $210 million contract over seven years with the Washington Nationals.

Scherzer won 92 games for Washington, including two more Cy Young Awards, and led the Nationals to a World Series win in 2019. The Nationals, not planning to sign the free agent after the 2021 season, traded him to the Los Angeles Dodgers in midseason. The thirty-six-year-old shows no sign of decline, winning seven games without a loss for the Dodgers in the second half of 2021.

The field Scherzer played high school baseball on is still used today. At the time of publication, he remains the only graduate of Parkway Central High to make the major leagues.

Cupples's Innovation

811 Spruce Street

Samuel Cupples moved to St. Louis in 1851 and established a wooden products business. With excellent business acumen, he built the business over the years and acquired a fortune. From 1888 to 1890, he built Cupples House, a Richardson Romanesque mansion at 3673 West Pine Mall. The forty-two-room home cost more than $150,000 to build, about $15,000,000 in 2021 dollars.

In the early 1890s, most St. Louis train tracks intersected in an area bounded by Seventh Street to the east, Eleventh Street to the west, Clark Avenue to the north and Poplar Street to the south. Transloading freight from one train to another required an army of horse-drawn dray carts. Cupples built twenty-two warehouses on the site in 1893 and 1894. The large brick Romanesque buildings, designed by famed St. Louis architects Eames and Young, were rugged and fire-resistant. Railway tracks underground connected the buildings and facilitated freight transfer. This

A 1910 postcard showing the Cupples warehouse complex. *St. Louis Public Library*.

The Westin Hotel. *Kathryn Flaspohler.*

innovative system increased the efficiency of goods handling and was the first of its type in the United States.

As technology changed, the importance of railroads declined while trucking increased. The Cupples warehouse complex was slowly abandoned. In the 1960s, several of the buildings were demolished to make room for Highway 40 (now Interstate 64). In 2001, another large warehouse was razed. Historic preservationists made serious efforts to save the remaining buildings.

The preservation efforts paid off. In 2001, a master plan was developed to save the remaining buildings. A set of four massive buildings near Busch Memorial Stadium underwent a $93 million project and were turned into the Westin Hotel. Several other warehouses have since become office space and apartments. The buildings sport restaurants and other retail spaces on their ground floors.

The Cardinals' new ballpark, Busch Stadium, is located directly across the street from the Weston. The hotel was already a favorite place to stay for many visiting baseball teams, and the new ballpark location cemented this reputation. It is an attractive location to stay for visiting fans for the same reasons. Patient autograph hawks can catch ballplayers walking from the hotel to the ballpark before a game.

JACK'S FINAL REST

2900 Sheridan Road

On September 17, 2001, a frail Jack Buck stepped to the microphone at Busch Stadium to welcome baseball back. Games had been canceled since the 9/11 terrorist attacks. Buck was suffering from the latter stages of Parkinson's disease, lung cancer, diabetes and other ailments, but he wanted to mark the occasion. Rising to the moment, the weakened broadcaster used a strong, emotional voice to read a poem he wrote and to speak to the fans and the large contingent of first responders.

One stanza of his poem, "We do not covet the possessions of others; / We are blessed with the bounty we share. / We have rushed to help other nations; / anything…anytime…anywhere," was a reflection of Buck's values. He was a generous person with his time and money, visiting hospitals and attending charitable functions, and he was a generous tipper. For his nearly fifty-year broadcasting career, he was a sought-after banquet speaker, making hundreds of appearances every year until his health declined.

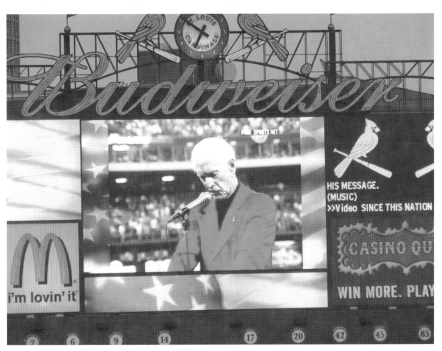

Jack Buck delivering his poem. *majorvols—Flikr.*

Left: Jack Buck's bust at Busch Stadium. *Kathryn Flaspohler*.

Below: Buck's monument at Jefferson Barracks National Cemetery. *Brian Flaspohler*.

The Cardinals honored their beloved broadcaster by including him in their roster of retired numbers and with a bust of him at Busch Stadium near the statue plaza. They retired his trademark call, which every Cardinal fan for generations wanted to hear at the end of a game: "That's a winner!"

Cardinal Nation celebrated his speech and the return of baseball. Buck answered the question about baseball returning: "I don't know about you, but as for me, the question has already been answered: Should we be here? Yes!"

This was one of Buck's last public appearances. His diseases continued to progress, and he died in June 2002. The World War II U.S. Army veteran, who was wounded near the Luddendorff Bridge at Remagen, was interred at Jefferson Barracks National Cemetery. His monument is in Section 85 (N38° 30.046', W90° 16.868'). Several other former major league players are also interred, including Chuck Diering and Bill Jennings.

Jefferson Barracks National Cemetery is one of the oldest national cemeteries. A military post was established there in 1826, and the first burial was a year later. The cemetery was formally dedicated as a national cemetery in 1866, and veterans from all U.S. wars, including three Revolutionary War veterans, and their spouses are interred here. Over two hundred thousand people are interred in the cemetery. There are also several military-themed museums on the Jefferson Barracks site open for visitors.

Sweet Lou Gives

1715 John Weber Drive

Say "Brock for Broglio," and many St. Louis Cardinal fans with an eye for team history will get a big grin. This 1964 trade with the Chicago Cubs proved to be one of the most lopsided in team history. In the six-player steal, the Cubs received Ernie Broglio, a former 21-game winner, and the Cardinals got Lou Brock, a young left fielder. Broglio would win 7 games for the Cubs over three seasons and then be out of baseball. Brock would play sixteen years for the Cardinals, join the 3,000-hit club and be elected to baseball's Hall of Fame in 1985, his first year of eligibility.

Brock's arrival sparked the Cardinals to a fast finish and a World Series win in 1964. His Redbird career highlights are many, including setting the season and career stolen base records (both since eclipsed by Rickey Henderson). He holds World Series records for batting average and stolen bases. He appeared in six All-Star Games and finished second in the National League

From left: Lou Brock, the author and Buck O'Neil at a baseball luncheon in the early 2000s. *Brian Flaspohler.*

Brock's statue in front of the Lou Brock Sports Complex. *Kathryn Flaspoher.*

Most Valuable Player voting in 1974. The Cardinals played in three World Series during Brock's career, winning two.

After his retirement from baseball, Brock stayed in St. Louis and became a great ambassador for the game. An intelligent and personable gentleman, the math major interacted with fans at many Cardinal events over the years. He established the Lou Brock Scholarship Foundation, which awarded scholarships to students of his alma mater, Southern University in Baton Rouge, Louisiana. After he married Jackie Brock, they became involved in Lindenwood University in St. Charles. He used his celebrity to raise money for the university's scholarship programs and other needs.

In 2005, Lindenwood built the Lou Brock Sports Complex, a baseball and softball venue on its campus. Brock was honored by the complex's name and a statue of him at the entrance. The state-of-the-art facilities have been selected several times to host college baseball and softball regional championship games. The statue captures Lou as he prepared for his signature hard slide. "Sweet Lou" was famous for sliding into bases aggressively and always feet first, to be ready to pop up and keep going if a ball got away.

Strawberry's Rehabilitation

900 Birdie Hills Road

Darryl and Tracy Strawberry.
Darryl Strawberry.

Darryl Strawberry was an amazing baseball talent. At twenty-one, he was named the National League Rookie of the Year. By twenty-four, he was a key player on the World Series champion New York Mets. New York papers declared him "The Straw That Stirs the Drink." By age twenty-nine, he had appeared in eight All-Star Games. That marked the height of his baseball prowess. He played eight more years, only reaching 100 games played for a season once. He fashioned a good major league career, clubbing 335 home runs. But most fans felt he squandered his baseball talents.

The Church on the Rock. *Kathryn Flaspohler.*

Drug and alcohol addictions led to Strawberry's rapid career decline. His addictions also were the cause of two divorces during his playing career, so his life was a mess on and off the baseball field. In 2000, a year after his playing career ended, he met his current wife, Tracy, at a narcotics center convention in Florida. She was a recovering drug addict, but he continued to fight his addictions over the next few years. She convinced him to leave his bad influences behind and move with her to St. Peters, Missouri, where the penniless couple lived in her parents' basement. They attended the Church on the Rock on Birdie Hills Road.

Strawberry found his salvation at the Church on the Rock and embraced sobriety. He paid off his debts and straightened out his life. Now he and Tracy, both ordained pastors, run their own ministry from their St. Charles home. Their mission is to teach people how to grow in their faith through step-by-step resources and daily encouragement.

The Church on the Rock is a nondenominational Christian church. It is an active congregation with weekly services broadcast on local television, Bible-study programs, children's events and small-group religious gatherings. Pastors David and Kim Blunt started the church in 1983 and have grown it into the large organization it is today.

THE FINAL GIFT

606 South Euclid Avenue

Jim Delsing was an average major league bench player for ten seasons. He had more than 400 at bats only three times in those years. The book on Delsing rated him a good-fielding center fielder with a below-average bat. The journeyman played for five different major league teams from 1948 to 1960 with his best playing season in 1953 for Detroit. He hit .288 with 11 home runs in 479 at bats, all career highs. He bounced around between organizations and spent time in the minor leagues. His baseball career consisted of 822 major league games and 1,227 games in the minors.

While with the Browns, Delsing was involved in an event cemented in baseball lore. Dwarf Eddie Gaedel pinch-hit in a game. After Gaedel drew a walk on four pitches and jogged to first, Delsing pinch-ran for him. In a classic baseball moment, as Delsing stood on first, Gaedel slapped his rear before heading to the dugout. Speaking of the moment, Delsing played it down, saying it happened quickly and the players did not consider it a historic feat, just another of Bill Veeck's promotions.

Delsing grew up in Wisconsin, but after he retired from baseball, he settled in St. Louis. A lifelong Catholic, he took a sales job with the *St. Louis Review*, the Catholic archdiocese newspaper. He worked thirty years for the paper before retiring in 1991. He gave time and resources to several Catholic charities over the years, including the St. Vincent de Paul Society, the St. Nicholas Food Pantry and the Ascension Altar Society.

Jim Delsing posing in his left-handed stance in the early 1950s. *Missouri Historical Society*.

Delsing and his wife, Roseanne, had five children, including professional golfer Jay Delsing. Jim attended St. Louis Browns Fan Club reunion luncheons for many years, always classy and appreciative that people remembered his career. When asked about his career, he said that putting on the major league uniform every day was the highlight.

Delsing died of cancer in 2006. In a final act of philanthropy, he donated his body to Washington University Medical

Washington University Medical School. *Kathryn Flaspohler.*

School. After the school finished with the body, the remains were cremated and buried in an undisclosed location. The excellent medical school on Euclid Avenue was ranked twelfth in the country by *US News and World Report* for medical research programs in 2021.

LESTER'S SPORTS BAR AND GRILL

9906 Clayton Road

Entrepreneur Lester Miller's life is a real Horatio Alger story. He grew up in New York City, selling newspapers outside of Broadway theaters during World War II. He left school as soon as he could, lying about his age to get his first real job as a traveling salesman when he was sixteen, hawking janitorial supplies.

Miller traveled to St. Louis as part of that job. He fell in love with the place, moving to the city and meeting and marrying his first wife when he was twenty-three. They had seven children. Miller got into the plastics industry, starting Contico, a plastics molding company, where he made his fortune. He sold divisions of his company for a total of $350 million in the late 1990s and early 2000s.

Miller took his fortune and bought real estate. One piece of his empire is Lester's Sports Bar and Grill on Clayton Road. The restaurant has a Stan Musial connection. Musial was Miller's friend for years, and Miller commissioned a slightly larger-than-life statue of Stan Musial to stand at

Some Bob Broeg SABR Chapter members with the Musial statue in front of Lester's after a Wednesday meeting. *Brian Flaspohler.*

Signed poster displayed in Lester's. Stan Musial had a very legible signature. *Brian Flaspohler.*

the entrance of the restaurant. Musial came to the restaurant opening in 2007 for the statue's unveiling and frequented the place when he was alive. The statue was produced by Harry Weber, the same person who sculpted the statues outside the new ballpark downtown.

Inside, a large number of signed baseballs and other sports memorabilia, including a poster signed by "The Man" to Miller, grace the space.

The menu has both deli-style sandwiches and smoked meats, both excellent choices when visiting. Plenty of TVs occupy every corner for sports viewing.

The Bob Broeg Chapter of the Society of American Baseball Research meets at Lester's at 5:30 p.m. on the first Wednesday of each month to talk baseball. One does not have to be a member to attend, though they should enjoy talking baseball. Look for a group of people sporting Cardinal paraphernalia sitting in the bar area.

JOSH HANCOCK'S ACCIDENT

Left Lane, Westbound Interstate 64,
before the Compton Avenue Exit (38A)

On April 28, 2007, Josh Hancock pitched three innings for the St. Louis Cardinals, allowing one run, in a blowout loss to the Chicago Cubs. After the game, he met with friends and had dinner at Mike Shannon's Steaks and Seafood.

At 12:41 a.m., Hancock was driving west on Interstate 64. He did not see the flatbed tow truck straddling the left lane and center shoulder, which had stopped to assist a Geo Prism that had struck the median. Hancock's rented Ford Explorer struck the truck's rear corner, with the driver's side of the Explorer taking the brunt of the damage. Hancock died instantly in the collision.

Right: Josh Hancock in 2006.
ShutUpJen, Flickr.

Below: The accident site today.
Brian Flaspohler.

The Cardinals game with the Cubs on Sunday was postponed while the Cardinal family processed the news. Team chairman Bill DeWitt II said, "The pain in our organization is unspeakable." Cardinals pitcher Braden Looper made a public statement for the players: "This has obviously been a difficult time for me and the Cardinals family. Josh was a great teammate and a great friend to everybody. He was a key part of our success last year and at the beginning of this year. We just have to get through this as a team and keep Josh's memory in our prayers and thoughts."

The accident investigation report said the tow truck had its emergency lights on. It reported that Hancock had a blood alcohol content of .157, nearly double the legal limit. He was driving thirteen miles per hour over the speed limit, was not wearing seat belts and was using his cellphone.

He made no effort to brake and only swerved right at the last split second before the collision. The tow truck driver was in his vehicle but was unhurt in the collision. The accident served as a catalyst for the organization to stop providing alcohol in the clubhouse. The shaken Cardinals went on to finish the season with a 78-84 record, their last losing season (through 2021).

The setting is unchanged today.

Hall of Fame Philanthropist

111 West Port Plaza Drive, #255

Jose Alberto Pujols Alcantara had one of the greatest runs to start a professional career of any player in baseball history. Known as Albert Pujols, his average season, for the eleven years he was a St. Louis Cardinal, was jaw-dropping. His triple slash line of batting average/on-base percentage/slugging percentage was a lofty .328/.420/.617. In his average season, he hammered 40 home runs, drove in 121 runs and scored 117 times. The lumbering slugger used baseball smarts and alertness to steal nearly 8 bases a year and take extra bases more than expected. He was named to nine All-Star teams, won the Rookie of the Year Award in 2001 and won three National League Most Valuable Player Awards. He led the Cardinals to World Series wins in 2006 and 2011.

Pujols went to the Los Angeles Angels starting in the 2012 season. No Cardinal player in any single season has come close to Albert's average season since he left the team. He is a future inner-circle Hall of Famer for his Cardinal years, no matter what the years since then have looked like. He was called "El Hombre" (Spanish for "The Man")—he stated that the moniker should be reserved for Stan Musial—and "The Machine" for his consistent great production.

Pujols is a dedicated family man to his wife and five children. He uses his wealth and fame to help the community. He established the Pujols Family Foundation, headquartered in the Westport Plaza complex, in 2005. The foundation's mission, taken from its website, is as follows: "a not-for-profit agency that exists to honor God and strengthen families through our works, deeds, and examples. We have sought to help those living with Down syndrome here at home and to improve the lives of the impoverished in the Dominican Republic."

Above: Albert Pujols receiving an award for his philanthropic work. *Luke X Martin*.

Right: The Pujols statue in front of the Westport Plaza tower, where his foundation is located. *Brian Flaspohler*.

Pujols was awarded baseball's Roberto Clemente Award in 2008. The annual award is given to the player who best demonstrates the values Clemente displayed in his commitment to community and understanding the value of helping others. Teammates nominate a player, and the league selects the winner from the thirty nominees.

Albert's wife, Deidre, shares his commitment. In 2010, he surprised her at Christmas with a massive diamond to celebrate their tenth wedding anniversary. When she saw the rock, she insisted he return it and instead put the money toward their charitable efforts.

The Pujols Family Foundation remains in Westport Plaza and continues to support Down syndrome families in the area. A larger-than-life-sized statue of him is located near the front of the Sheraton Chalet Hotel.

The Voice of the Cardinals

1220 Olive Street, Suite 300

KMOX Radio, except for brief periods from 1949 to 1953 and 2006 to 2010, has broadcast St. Louis Cardinal baseball games since 1928. The strong nighttime signal from the station and St. Louis's geographic location ensured legions of people in western, plains and midwestern states became Cardinal fans, because they could hear the games.

A group of St. Louis businessmen started the radio station in the early 1920s. They wanted the call letters KVSL, for "Voice of St. Louis," but they also applied for KMO. Those call letters were in use, but the station was granted KMOX, for Missouri (MO) and Christmas (X), since the station began broadcasting on Christmas Eve, 1925. In 1927, CBS bought the station and applied for permission to build a fifty-thousand-watt transmitter. This was granted, and KMOX became one of the nation's clear-channel stations.

It began sports broadcasting, airing the 1926 World Series games between St. Louis and the New York Yankees. In 1928, the station broadcast Cardinals and Browns games, as did other stations in the St. Louis area. In those heady days, there were no exclusive rights to the games, and any station could broadcast them. When the St. Louis Cardinals began selling rights in 1949, another station won the bid, but KMOX bought the rights in 1954.

Left: The Mart Building (now called the Robert E. Young Federal Building) in 1940, when KMOX was there. *St. Louis Public Library*.

Right: KMOX's current home is on the third floor of the Park Pacific Building. *Kathryn Flaspohler*.

In 1955, Robert Hyland became the station's general manager. He made the decision to go to an all-talk format, the first station in the United States to do so. Sports programming was a big part of the strategy. Hyland built the station up from a strong position to one of the most respected and powerful in the industry.

KMOX was the home for many of the great broadcasters in Cardinals history. Harry Caray, Gabby Street, Jack Buck, Bob Costas, Dizzy Dean, Joe Buck and Mike Shannon all broadcast for the station. The current lead Cardinal television announcer, Dan McLaughlin, started at the station.

The station's studios are now located in the Park Pacific Building on Olive Street. They moved in 2012 after many years at One Memorial Way. The twenty-two-story art deco building was erected for the Missouri Pacific Railroad in the late 1920s and originally called the Missouri Pacific Building. Designed by architecture firm Mauran, Russell & Crowell, the building used setbacks, a style pioneered in New York City to allow light to reach the street, in anticipation of other high-rise buildings being erected nearby. Those structures were never built. The railroad occupied the building until 2005.

In 2011, a developer purchased the building and renovated much of it into apartments. Office space for KMOX and other tenants is still provided on the lower floors.

Hall of Fame Cemetery

740 North Mason Road

A number of baseball Hall of Famers are buried in the St. Louis area. George Sisler, "Cool Papa" Bell, Joe Medwick and Red Schoendienst found their final rest in the area, though they are in different cemeteries. One cemetery in the area contains two Hall of Famers, Bellerive Heritage Gardens in Creve Coeur. There are four major leaguers interred here, two of whom have been awarded Major League Baseball's highest honor.

Stan Musial, the undisputed greatest player in St. Louis Cardinals' franchise history, died on January 19, 2013. On January 24, a public visitation was held at the Cathedral Basilica of St. Louis, where he lay in state. Thousands of fans braved extreme cold in the long line outside the cathedral to pay their respects. A private funeral service was held two days later, and he was temporarily buried in the cemetery mausoleum. At a later date, he and his wife's remains were moved to their final resting place in Section 6. They are the only two people in this section, numbered to match

Stan Musial's gravesite. *Kathryn Flaspohler.*

Lou Brock's resting place. *Kathryn Flaspohler.*

his uniform number. The Man's large red-granite monument is near the southeast corner of the cemetery (N38° 39.997', W90° 27.883'), with a bench nearby to allow the visitor quiet appreciation of his achievements both on and off the baseball diamond.

Base stealer Lou Brock died on September 6, 2020, after suffering from diabetes and blood cancer. He was living in St. Charles at the time of his death but had lived in Ladue for many years. There was a public visitation for him at Layne Renaissance Chapel on September 11. Two days later, a processional was held, beginning with a wreath-laying at his statue at Lindenwood University and ending at Greater Grace Church in St. Charles for a private service. After the service, the processional went to his statue at Busch Stadium, where the family laid a second wreath, then proceeded to the cemetery. His remains are in the cemetery mausoleum. Inside the main entrance, his remains are to the right, about eight feet above the floor (N38° 39.348', W90° 27.324').

Bellerive Heritage Gardens, founded in 1925, is a nondenominational cemetery. It has a different look than the typical St. Louis–area cemetery. The grounds have fewer vertical monuments. Many graves are marked with flat stones, and the grounds are laid out to encourage walking and contemplation.

Uncle Charlie

2100 Brook Hill Court

In December 2003, the St. Louis Cardinals traded J.D. Drew and Eli Marrero to the Atlanta Braves for Ray King, Jason Marquis and a minor leaguer. The trade turned out well for St. Louis. That minor leaguer, Adam Wainwright, possessed one of the best curveballs in major league history. The curveball, known as "Uncle Charlie" in baseball slang, provided Wainwright with a great nickname, particularly as he has aged into his final years in the sport.

Wainwright broke into the majors in 2005, pitching two relief innings late in the year. The Cardinals used him in middle relief in 2006 to soften his entry into the majors. However, during the last week of the regular season, the team used him as the closer, and he recorded the last outs in the National League Championship Series against the Mets and in the World Series against the Detroit Tigers.

Beginning in 2007, Wainwright moved into a starting role and pitched well, winning 64 games, including 20 wins in the 2010 season. He missed 2011 after undergoing Tommy John surgery, but the Cardinals, understanding his value, exercised the option on his contract.

In 2008, Wainwright, earning a modest salary by baseball standards, purchased a home on Brook Hill Court in Chesterfield, a western suburb of St. Louis. He and his family resided there until 2016, when they moved to accommodate his large family of four daughters and a son.

Wainwright came back strong from his 2011 injury. He won 19 games in 2013 and 20 in 2014 but suffered another injury, missing most of 2015. After that season, he struggled. As his health returned, he had a career revival. As a thirty-nine-year-old in 2021, he won 17 games, leading the Cardinal

Adam Wainwright demonstrating his curveball. *John Max Mena.*

Wainwright's former Chesterfield, Missouri home. *Kathryn Flaspohler.*

pitching staff. Through the 2021 season, he and catcher Yadier Molina have started 304 games together, the fourth most by any battery in history.

Wainwright has amassed an impressive 184-105 regular-season record for the St. Louis Cardinals over his career through 2021. He is only the second Cardinal pitcher to strike out 2,000 batters, behind Bob Gibson. As soon as he retires, he will be inducted into the Cardinals Hall of Fame.

His former home in Chesterfield is still a private residence in a subdivision.

BEEP BALL

3300 Hickory Street

Modifying a sport in which the main objective is to hit a round ball with a round bat squarely, to allow visually impaired people to take part seems like a daunting task. In the early 1970s, a group of people came together to try to overcome obstacles and build a version of baseball for the visually impaired.

The designed game is different from baseball, of course, but it contains the primary elements of a batter trying to hit a ball, fielders trying to get control of the batted ball and base running. The game is played on a grass

Sighted pitcher tossing to a visually impaired batter on the St. Louis University Medical Stadium field. *Kathryn Flaspohler.*

field with six fielders, typically three infielders and three outfielders. The pitcher and catcher are sighted and on the same team as the batter. The ball is an oversized softball, modified with a beeping mechanism inside. There are two bases, each one hundred feet from home plate in the positions roughly equivalent to first and third base. The bases are foam columns with a mechanism that emits a steady tone when the base is activated.

The batter receives four strikes and must swing at every pitch. If the ball travels less than forty feet, it is a foul. When the batter strikes the ball, a sighted base operator activates a switch for one of the two bases. The batter runs toward the tone. The fielders attempt to corral the beeping ball, with the spotters on their team calling out the general location (numbered 1–6) of the balls. If the fielder secures the ball before the runner reaches the base, the runner is out. Otherwise, it is scored a run. No other base running occurs.

The game has six innings, and all visually impaired players wear blindfolds. This ensures that people who are legally blind but still have some vision take part on an equal basis. Because the pitcher is on the same team as the batter, the goal is to throw the same way each time, and the batters try to swing with consistency. Timing is everything to allow solid contact. Typical strategy in

Left: Baserunner heading toward his base. *Kathryn Flaspohler*.

Right: The Gateway Archers' Liam McCoy in full uniform, pads and blindfold goggles. *Kathryn Flaspohler*.

the field is to dive down horizontally and cover ground so the ball will strike the fielder. The baserunner's methodology is to run hard toward the base and throw their arms out wide to ensure contact.

The National Beep Ball Association was organized in 1976 and holds a world series tournament each year. St. Louis has had various teams participate over the years. Currently, the Gateway Archers is the competitive local team. Archer home games are played at the St. Louis University Medical Stadium on Hickory Street. The team finished ninth in the 2021 Beep Ball World Series in Indiana after entering the tournament seeded seventeenth.

Busch Stadium

700 Clark Avenue

In the 1780s, when St. Louis was no more than a three-by-nine-block area running north–south along the Mississippi River, Joseph Motard built a mill to process the colonists' grain. The French colonists' children, less than twenty years later, congregated near the mill and played ball there, using the mill as a backstop of sorts. To be clear, they did not play baseball. The game must have been one of a couple different bat-and-ball games popular in France at the time. Motard's Mill occupied the site where the current St. Louis Cardinals play baseball, the new Busch Stadium. It is comforting to know that the history of bat-and-ball games in this location goes back to the founding of the city.

The multipurpose Busch Memorial Stadium was showing its age by 2000, and the St. Louis Cardinals stepped up lobbying for a new stadium. There was talk of moving west to St. Louis County or across the river to Illinois. Cooler heads eventually prevailed, and a site adjacent to Busch Memorial Stadium was selected.

In fact, the stadiums were more than adjacent; they overlapped. Construction on the new stadium began in January 2004. Two-thirds of the stadium was built by the end of the 2005 season, while the old stadium was still in use. The Cardinals did not make it easy on the construction crews. In 2005, the team won the division and advanced to the National League Championship Series, losing in six games. Demolition of the old

Construction of the new Busch Stadium. *David K. Staub*.

Statue plaza. *Kathryn Flaspohler.*

Ballpark Village entrance. *Kathryn Flaspohler.*

Busch began on November 3, 2005, but not before nearly everything of value, from kitchen equipment to seats to signs to the clubhouse urinal, was removed from the stadium and sold to fans.

By the start of the 2006 season, the old stadium was gone and the new venue was ready for fans, although additional seating needed to be completed. Work continued through the season. The team won the World Series in the inaugural year of the park, a fitting way to christen their new home. They added another World Series win in 2011.

The new stadium, designed by HOK Sport and built by Hunt Construction Group, cost $365 million. The brick façade evokes St. Louis architecture, and some of the decorative features reflect surrounding structures, such as Eads Bridge. The Cardinals moved Stan Musial's iconic statue to its current location outside of the third-base gates and began populating the area northwest of the stadium with statues carved by Harry Weber honoring Cardinal greats and, in a nod to St. Louis baseball history, George Sisler and James "Cool Papa" Bell.

Part of the overall project was future construction of Ballpark Village, an entertainment venue occupying the space left by the old ballpark. It took several years for financing and construction to start, but now Ballpark

Busch Stadium. *Kathryn Flaspohler.*

Village is largely complete. The complex includes restaurants, shops, the Cardinals Hall of Fame and Museum, an apartment complex and a rooftop viewing area reminiscent of Wrigley Field's rooftop viewing. A giant screen inside Ballpark Village allows sports fans to get their fill year-round.

Busch Stadium has a great skyline view of the Gateway Arch and the city. It has been criticized by some for limited family attractions within the park, but the focus here is on baseball, as it should be. It is a great place to see a game, and the team has a history of contending every season, keeping the forty-five thousand seats filled.

Soviet-Era Artist Carved "The Man"!?

Eighth Street and Spruce Street

A casual visitor to St. Louis heads to the stadium from the west, going down one of the tree-named streets that run east and west. If they walk on Spruce, they will see the stadium in the distance, along with a statue outside the third-base gates. The eight-foot pedestal sports an eleven-foot-high statue. As they gaze at the top-heavy batter poised to swing a pencil bat, they wonder who this represents. They question one of the ubiquitous fans in red and are gobsmacked by the answer: "Why, Stan Musial of course."

In the 1960s, sportswriter Bob Broeg and others began raising money for a Musial statue. They wanted a statue based on a drawing by Amadee Wohlschlaeger, longtime sports cartoonist for the *St. Louis*

The Man's statue. *Kathryn Flaspohler.*

Post-Dispatch. Wohlschlaeger imagined Musial signing a scorecard for a young fan. Musial loved the concept. The group was not able to raise enough money, and the idea languished.

Raymond Tucker, the St. Louis mayor, raised the money and made sure his friend, former Washington University fine arts professor Carl Mose, got the commission to design the statue. Mose designed the left-handed batter

Stan Musial demonstrating his stance. *Missouri Historical Society.*

shown today. Mose was a modernist and likely did not have the skill set required to craft a lifelike rendering. Musial reviewed early models and was not happy. "He made me all bulky. I tried to get him to change it, but he just never would....He never did get it right."

But Stan was nothing if not gracious. In 1968, when the statue was unveiled at its original location, the intersection of Broadway and Walnut outside Busch Memorial Stadium, he was there and gave an emotional speech. With a straight face, he noted that the sculpture came close to capturing him.

Despite its failure to resemble the actual Stan Musial, the statue served as a meeting point for generations of Cardinal fans. In the era before cellphones, many baseball game plans would end with someone saying, "Meet me at the Musial statue." The pedestal has "Musial" on one side of the base and, on the other side, the Ford Frick quote from Musial's retirement ceremony: "Here Stands Baseball's Perfect Warrior...Here Stands Baseball's Perfect Knight."

Left: Fans meeting up at the Musial statue before a game. *Kathryn Flaspohler*.

Right: The Harry Weber statue of Stan Musial. *Kathryn Flaspohler*.

The statue was moved to its current location when the new stadium was built. The eighty-seven-year-old Musial was in attendance at the rededication and wryly noted, "I'm so frail now because I hit too many triples." Wohlschlaeger's original design was sculpted by Harry Weber and placed outside of the Missouri Sports Hall of Fame in Springfield in 2005. A smaller statue by Weber of Musial is in the Cardinal plaza of statues. That statue captures Musial at the end of his swing, a beautiful rendering of "The Man" in action.

6

SUGGESTED TOUR ROUTES

THE MAJOR LEAGUE BALLPARKS TOUR

St. Louis is home to nine different locations where major league games were played, including two places where the St. Louis Stars played. Following this suggested route takes about three hours, not counting the time to tour the current stadium complex. The tour starts at the first ballpark to host a professional league game in St. Louis and ends at the current Cardinals stadium and Ballpark Village.

Start at a small parking lot at 3201 Chouteau. Looking north, note the large building in the distance. This building occupies the site where the first major league game was played in the city. Go left out of the lot and left at Compton. As you drive over the railroad tracks, note that home plate of Red Stockings Park (page 24) sat north of the railroad tracks. Take a left at Spruce. The second left is the main entrance to the Metro Bi-State facility. A historical marker is on the left under the trees.

Leave the facility going right on Spruce. At Compton, go left. After crossing Highway 64, turn right onto Market. On your left is the site of Stars Park (page 78). The St. Louis Stars, anchored by "Cool Papa" Bell, won three pennants in four years at this site, now occupied by the Harris Stowe State University baseball field. Turn around and park in front of the baseball facility. A historical marker here contains park information.

Go west on Market. Drive past Compton, then merge onto Forest Park Parkway. Take the first exit (Grand). Go right on Grand, then right on Laclede. Take the first right into the parking lot in front of the West

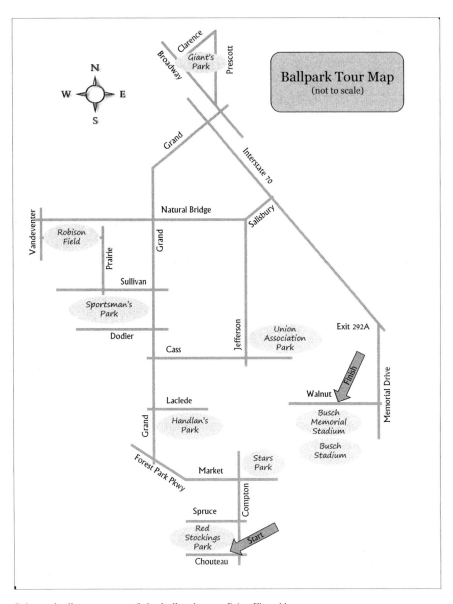

Schematic diagram map of the ballpark tour. *Brian Flaspohler*.

Marchetti Tower. Here is the site of Handlan's Park (page 53), home of the St. Louis Terriers.

Go left out of the lot. Take a right at Grand, then proceed about a mile, turning right onto Cass. In three-fourths of a mile, take a left on Jefferson.

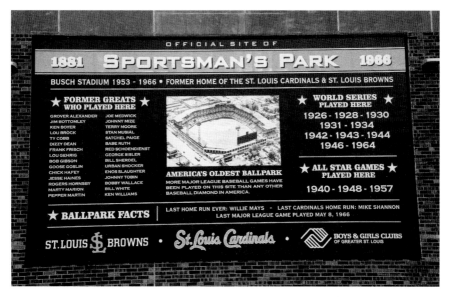

Sportsman's Park billboard displayed on the Herbert Hoover Boys and Girls Club. *Kathryn Flaspohler.*

Immediately to your right is the site of the St. Louis Maroons' home field, Union Association Park (page 37). The Maroons went 94-19 in their only season in the Union Association, the best record a St. Louis team has ever had in any major league.

Continue north on Jefferson for a mile until the roundabout. Take the left-most exit to Natural Bridge Avenue. Go left on Grand, then right on Dodier. The Herbert Hoover Boys and Girls Club sits on the site of legendary Sportsman's Park (page 27). To go onto the historic field, enter the clubhouse building and ask to go out on the field. Do not be fooled by the baseball field west of the complex. That is a modern Little League field, not the site of Sportsman's Park.

Take Dodier east to Grand. Go left on Grand, then left on Sullivan and right on Prairie. Take the fourth left (unmarked). This alley goes behind Beaumont High School. The alley marks the center of Robison Field (page 45), the outfield being where the track is now. The Cardinals played here from 1893 to 1920.

At the end of the alley, turn right onto Vandeventer, then right onto Natural Bridge Avenue. At the roundabout, turn onto Salisbury. Stay on Salisbury for two-thirds of a mile, then merge onto Interstate 70 west. Take the Grand exit. Go left on Broadway. In about three-fourths of a mile, turn right on Clarence. This desolate chunk of concrete wasteland marks the location of Giants' Park (page 68), the home of the St. Louis Giants and the second incarnation of the St. Louis Stars.

Continue on Clarence and go right on Prescott. Join Broadway southbound, then turn right on Grand and merge onto Highway 70 going east. In about two miles, exit at Convention Plaza (exit 292A). Take a right onto Walnut. Pull into Ballpark Village's parking lot on the left. Busch Memorial Stadium (page 150) and Busch Stadium (page 191) sites are here. Enjoy the current epicenter of St. Louis major league baseball. This is a perfect place to walk around and get lunch in or around Ballpark Village, visit the Cardinals Hall of Fame and Museum, shop at the team store for Cardinal memorabilia and enjoy the statues of the St. Louis baseball greats.

Hall of Famer Gravesite Tour

Over 250 players, executives, umpires and other baseball figures are buried in the St. Louis area. Among this number are six Hall of Fame players, one Hall of Fame broadcaster, one Hall of Fame writer and one "should be in the Hall of Fame" owner. This route visits those nine people interred in eight cemeteries (two players are in Bellerive Heritage Gardens) and takes about four hours, depending on traffic.

The starting point is Bellefontaine Cemetery at 4947 West Florissant Avenue. The Cardinals' first owner, Chris von der Ahe (page 32), is here. He is not in the Hall of Fame but has a case because of his pioneering innovations. Enter the cemetery from the main gate on West Florissant. Go right on Fountain, left on Vale, right on Lake and left on Memorial. His impressive statue and monument is on the left (N38° 41.396', W90° 13.733').

Exit Bellefontaine Cemetery and go left on West Florissant Avenue. Follow the signs and take Interstate 70 west. Go two miles to the Lucas and Hunt exit and turn left. After about a mile, the entrance to St. Peter's Cemetery is on the right. In the cemetery, turn left, left and left again to James "Cool Papa" Bell's grave (page 97). It is at N38° 41.242', W90° 17.653' on the right side of the road.

Exit St. Peter's and take Lucas and Hunt Road back to I-70. Go west for five miles, then take Interstate 270 toward Memphis. Take the Olive Road exit and turn right. At Mason Road, go left. Enter Bellerive Heritage Gardens cemetery at the second entrance on the left. Follow the road signs toward the chapel. Park at the large mausoleum and enter the doors. Lou Brock (pages

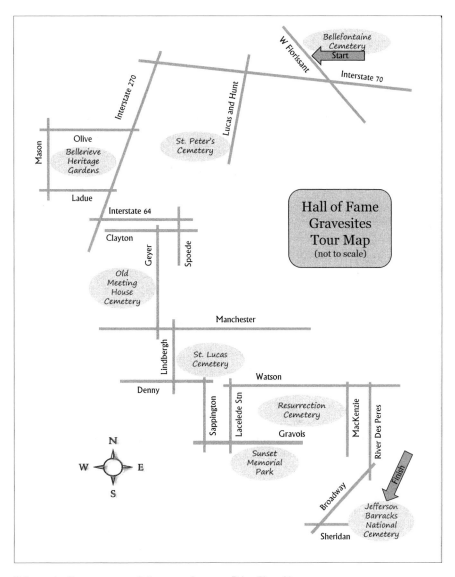

Schematic diagram map of the gravesite tour. *Brian Flaspohler.*

173, 186) is on the right side, six locations in and four high (N38° 39.967', W90° 27.900'). Exiting the mausoleum, go right. Go right into the Reflection Gardens area. Stan Musial (pages 125, 129, 186) has a large red monument on the right side of the road (N38° 39.991', W90° 27.883').

Exit the cemetery and go left on Mason Road. Turn left on Ladue Road. At Interstate 270, go south. In one mile, take Interstate 64 east. In one mile, turn right on Spoede Road, then right on Clayton Road and left on North Geyer Road. In one-half mile, a white historic church is on the right. Park in the small turn-in to the right immediately after the church. George Sisler (page 75) is in the columbarium at N38° 37.358', W90° 25.211'. His son, major leaguer Dick Sisler, is very close in the same columbarium.

Continue south on Geyer Road. In a mile and a half, turn left at Manchester Road. At Lindbergh Boulevard, turn right. Go four miles, then turn left on Denny Road. St. Lucas Cemetery is on the left. Park at the first tree on the left. Joe Medwick (page 95) is interred here at N38° 32.246', W90° 23.322'.

Exit the cemetery and go left on Denny. Turn right on Sappington Road, then left on Gravois Road. Go one mile, then enter Sunset Memorial Park on the right. Go right, then right again. Sportswriter Bob Broeg (page 61), recipient of the J.G. Taylor Spink Award, is at N38° 32.889', W90° 20.515'. As an added bonus, visit the Busch family burial ground in the copse of trees north of Broeg's grave. Cardinal owner August Busch II (page 135) rests at N38° 32.903', W90° 20.532'.

Exit the cemetery and go left on Gravois Road, then right on Laclede Station Road. In one mile, turn right on Watson Road. In about a mile, turn

Bob Broeg's gravesite. *Kathryn Flaspohler.*

Red Schoendienst's family monument. *Kathryn Flaspohler.*

right on MacKenzie Road. Resurrection Cemetery's entrance is on the right. At the first fork, go right, then take the second left. Red Schoendienst (page 141) is left of the road at N38° 34.514', W90° 19.381'.

Exit the cemetery, go left on MacKenzie, right on Watson and right on River Des Peres Boulevard. The signage for River Des Peres is poor; turn before the river. Stay on the road (it changes names) for about three miles to Broadway. Go right, then turn left on Sheridan Road. Enter Jefferson Barracks National Cemetery on Jefferson Boulevard. At the roundabout, take Flagstaff Drive. Take a left on Circle Drive, and Jack Buck (pages 144, and 171) is on the left at N38° 30.046', W90° 16.868'. His monument is marked "John Buck," so watch for that. For the explorer, there are nice views back toward the city and over the Mississippi River from the higher points in the cemetery.

THE HISTORIC BUILDINGS TOUR

St. Louis, despite the removal of the original downtown core to install the Gateway Arch, has a number of baseball-related historic buildings worth visiting. The ten buildings on this list were all erected before 1930 and show architecture typical of the city. This tour takes about two hours, not counting time spent touring the Anheuser-Busch Brewery. I recommend doing it on a weekday, because the Security Building and Civil Courts Building are open, allowing a visitor to see the inside lobby spaces.

Start at the parking lot northwest of 956 Hamilton Avenue. The Hamilton Hotel (page 63), built for the 1904 World's Fair, is now an apartment complex. Exit the parking lot to the right and go left on Maple. Take a right at Goodfellow, then turn left at Delmar and right on Kingshighway. Turn left on Forest Park Parkway. Follow the signs to merge on Market. Turn left on Compton and right on Laclede Avenue. The main Harris Stowe University Building is the historic Vashon High School (page 89).

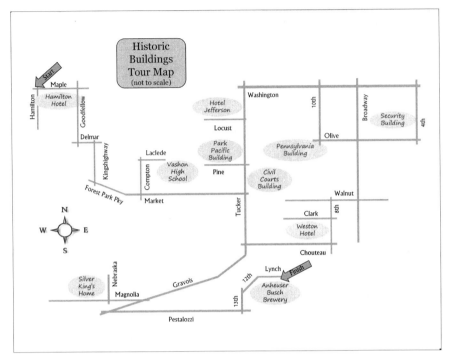

Schematic diagram map of the historic building tour. *Brian Flaspohler.*

Take Laclede west. Go left at Compton, then turn left at Market. Turn left at Tucker. The Civil Courts Building (page 113) is on the right. In two blocks, the Park Pacific Building (page 184) is on the left. Park is the area for the Civil Courts Building lobby, or continue north on Tucker.

In two blocks, the Hotel Jefferson (page 80) is on the left. This building is currently vacant and cannot be accessed. Continue to Washington and turn right, then turn right at Tenth. In three blocks, look right for the Pennsylvania Building (page 39). If it is lunchtime, stop and eat at Jack Patrick's in the Pennsylvania Building for some typical bar food.

Turn left at Olive. Go five blocks, then turn left on Fourth. The Security Building (page 57) is on the left. The lobby rotunda is nicely restored and worth a look.

Turn left on Washington and left on Broadway. Go right on Walnut and left on Eighth. The Westin Hotel (page 169) is on the right. Other restored Cupples warehouses are west of the Westin.

Go south on Eighth, right on Chouteau and left on Tucker. Stay on Tucker until it goes past the highway interchange and becomes Gravois. Take a right

Left: One of the twenty-feet-tall black marble columns in the Civil Courts Building that contributed to the cost overruns during construction. *Brian Flaspohler.*

Below: A view of the restored lobby of the Security Building. *Brian Flaspohler.*

on Magnolia (the street after Lynch). After Nebraska, Silver King's home is on the right (page 41).

Turn around. Take Magnolia east. Go right at Gravois, then left on Pestalozzi (before the Quiktrip). Stay on Pestalozzi and cross Highway 55. Turn left on Thirteenth and right on Twelfth. Enter the Anheuser-Busch (page 135) parking lot. This is the end of the driving tour. Make sure to take the brewery tour to get the best views of the many historic buildings in the Anheuser-Busch complex. After your free beer tasting, lunch is available at the brewery beer garden restaurant.

BIBLIOGRAPHY

Books and Journals

Achorn, Edward. *The Summer of Beer and Whiskey*. New York: Public Affairs, 2013.

Alexander, Charles. *Rogers Hornsby*. New York: Henry Holt and Company, 1995.

Brennan, Charlie. *Here's Where*. St. Louis: Missouri Historical Society Press, 2006.

Broeg, Bob. *Redbirds: A Century of Cardinals Baseball*. Marceline, MO: Walsworth Publishing Company, 1992.

Cash, Jon David. *Before They Were Cardinals*. Columbia: University of Missouri Press, 2002.

————. *Boom and Bust in St. Louis*. Jefferson, NC: MacFarland & Company, 2020.

Creamer, Robert W. *Babe: The Legend Comes to Life*. New York: Penguin Books, 1983.

Garagiola, Joe. *Baseball Is a Funny Game*. New York: Harper Collins, 1990.

Giglio, James N. *Musial: From Stash to Stan the Man*. Columbia: University of Missouri Press, 2001.

Huhn, Rick. *The Sizzler*. Columbia: University of Missouri Press, 2004.

Lampe, Anthony B. "The Background of Professional Baseball in St. Louis." *Missouri Historical Society Bulletin* (October 1950).

Lowry, Philip J. *Green Cathedrals*. New York: Walker Publishing Company, 2006.

Smith, Irene Sanford. *Ferguson: A City and Its People*. Ferguson, MO: Ferguson Historical Society, 1976.

St. Louis City and County directories and phone books.

Wagenheim, Kal. *Babe Ruth: His Life and Legend*. New York: Open Road Media, 2014.

Wheatley, Ed. *Baseball in St. Louis: From Little Leagues to Major Leagues*. St. Louis, MO: Reedy Press, 2020.

NEWSPAPER ARCHIVES

Daily Missouri Republican (St. Louis, MO)
Los Angeles Times
Riverfront Times (St. Louis, MO)
St. Louis Argus
St. Louis Globe-Democrat
St. Louis Magazine
St. Louis Post-Dispatch
St. Louis Republic
St. Louis Star-Times
The Sporting News
Washington Post

WEBSITES

Ancestry.com. https://www.ancestry.com.

Ashwill, Gary. Agate Type. https://agatetype.typepad.com/agate_type.

Coll, Tom. Joe Fassi Sausage and Sandwich Factory. https://www.joefassisandwiches.com/#home-section.

Forman, Sean. Baseball Reference. https://www.baseball-reference.com.

Gorton, Peter. John Donaldson Network. http://johndonaldson.bravehost.com/index.html.

Groth, Mark. St. Louis City Talk. http://www.stlouiscitytalk.com.

Hammerman, Harley. Lost Tables. https://losttables.com.

History's Homes. http://www.historyshomes.com/detail.cfm?id=491.

Kittel, Jeff. This Game of Games. http://thisgameofgames.com.

Lafayette Square Restoration Committee. Lafayette Square. https:// lafayettesquare.org.

Lynch, Mike. Seamheads. https://seamheads.com/blog.

McCray, Larry. Protoball. https://protoball.org.

Missouri Department of Natural Resources. https://dnr.mo.gov.

Missouri State Historical Preservation Office. Mound City on the Mississippi. http://dynamic.stlouis-mo.gov/history/histstruct.cfm.

Naffziger, Chris. St. Louis Patina. https://stlouispatina.com.

Palermo, Tom. "The World's First Modern Sports Bar." When It Was a Game. http://www.whenitwasagame.net/story_pages/osb.html.

Perry, Todd. Pujols Family Foundation. https://www.pujolsfamilyfoundation. org.

Powers, Robert. Built St. Louis. http://www.builtstlouis.net.

Schrader Funeral Home. "Our Story." https://www.schrader.com.

St. Louis City Property Records. https://www.stlouis-mo.gov/data/address-search.

St. Louis County Property Records. https://revenue.stlouisco.com/IAS.

Wikipedia. https://www.wikipedia.org.

SOCIETY FOR AMERICAN BASEBALL RESEARCH (HTTPS://SABR.ORG)

Armour, Mark. "Sam Breadon."

Bohn, Matt. "Harry Caray."

Corbett, Warren. "Earl Weaver."

———. "Joe Garagiola."

———. "Marty Marion."

Daly, Jon. "Billy Southworth."

Faber, Charles. "Joe Medwick."

Ferkovich, Scott. "Sportsman's Park."

Flaspohler, Brian. "Bill Jenning."

———. "Bob Broeg."

———. "Jack Gleason."

———. "Patsy's Tebeau."

Forr, James. "Bob Prince."

Grillo, Jerry. "Johnny Mize."

Hirsch, Paul. "Jerry Reuss."

Hurd, Jay. "Quincy Trouppe."

Lamb, Bill. "Pat Hynes."

Lamberty, Bill. "George Sisler."

Lokemoen, Kristen. "Jack Buck."

———. "Red Schoendienst."

McCann, Kevin. "Mike Shannon."

McCue, Andy. "Branch Rickey."

Nowlin, Bill. "John Tobin."

Riechers, Carl. "Hank Arft."

Rogers, C. Paul, III. "Rogers Hornsby."

Sargent, Jim. "Jim Delsing."

Sloope, Terry. "Bob Gibson."

———. "Curt Flood."

Stahl, John. "Johnny Keane."

Steinberg, Steve. "Robert Hedges."

Tan, Cecilia. "Elston Howard."

Thomas, Joan M. "Helene Britton."

———. "Red Stockings Park."

———. "Robison Field."

———. "St. Louis Unions Park."

———. "Union Base Ball Park."

Wancho, Joseph. "Dizzy Dean."

———. "Gabby Street."

———. "Luke Sewell."

Wilke, Dave. "James 'Cool Papa' Bell."

Williams, Dave. "Yogi Berra."

Wolf, Gregory. "Heinie Meine."

———. "Nate Colbert."

———. "Silver King."

INTERVIEWS

Berkovich, Ari. Interview with author, August 13, 2021.

Coll, Tom. Interview with author, September 9, 2021.

Finch, Brian. Tour of St. Louis Cardinals Hall of Fame and Museum, March 18, 2018.

Grbic, Ermina. Interview with author, August 28, 2021.

Reuss, Jerry. Presentation to Bob Broeg SABR Chapter, April 12, 2021.

Riechers, Carl. Interview with author, August 20, 2021.

Sheinbein, Barbara. Presentation at James Rygelski Research Conference, September 18, 2021.

Taaffe, Norma Kuebler. Interview with author, September 2, 2021.

INDEX

A

ABC Park 10
Addie Avenue 7
All-Star Awards 157
Ames, Leon 63
Anheuser-Busch Brewery 135
Anheuser, Eberhard 135
Antonelli, Johnny 138
Arft, Henry 134
Ashland Avenue 46, 63

B

Bailey Farm Dairy 141
Ballpark Village 152, 161, 194
Ball, Philip 34, 53
Bartmer Avenue 101
Beaumont High School 18, 47,
    117, 127, 163
Bellefontaine Cemetery 31, 32, 37,
    60, 136

Bellerive Heritage Gardens 186
Bell, James "Cool Papa" 78, 89,
    97, 186, 194
Bergmann, Erma 115
Berra, Yogi 91, 102, 119, 146,
    149, 166, 167
Birdie Hills Road 175
Bishop, Campbell Orrick 24, 34
Blackwell, Charlie 69
Blattner, Buddy 146
Blong, Joe 37
Bonds, Barry 82
Bottomley, Jim 101
Bradsby, Frank 34
Breadon, Sam 47, 67, 82, 101,
    128, 129
Bresnahan, Roger 56
Brett, George 157
Britton, Helene Hathaway 55, 67
Broadway 68, 141, 196
Brock, Lou 149, 155, 166, 173, 187
Broeg, Bob 61, 84, 96, 117, 180,
    195

Broglio, Ernie 173
Brook Hill Court 188
Buck, Jack 144, 146, 159, 161,
        166, 171, 185
Buck, Joe 163, 185
Burnes, Bob 61
Busch, Adolphus 32, 135
Busch, August, II 67, 117, 122,
        132, 136, 149, 150, 155
Buschmann, Matt 165
Busch Memorial Stadium 24, 28, 29,
        123, 138, 151, 170, 192, 196
Busch Stadium 152, 170, 171,
        173, 187, 191
Byerly, Bill 97

C

Calvary Cemetery 34, 51, 66, 91
Caray, Harry 86, 95, 114, 132,
        144, 185
Cardinals Hall of Fame and
        Museum 152, 195
Cass Avenue 37
Cates Avenue 51
Charleston, Oscar 69
Chase Park Plaza Hotel 131
Chestnut Street 73
Childress Avenue 125, 129
Chippewa Street 129
Chouteau Avenue 119
Christian Brothers College High
        School 159
Church on the Rock 176
Church Street 71
Civil Courts Building 114
Clarence Avenue 68, 138
Clark Avenue 169, 191

Clay Street 71
Clayton Avenue 86
Clayton Road 102, 154, 163, 179
Cobb, Ty 76, 105
Colbert, Nate 138
Comiskey, Charles 30
Compton Avenue 24, 78, 180
Costas, Bob 185
Cuthbert, Ned 30

D

Dale Avenue 109
Dark, Alvin 142
Dean, Dizzy 95, 165, 185
Dean, Paul 96, 165
Delmar Boulevard 165
Delsing, Jim 177
Denny Road 95
Des Peres Avenue 165
DeWitt, Bill, II 67, 138, 181
Dickey, Bill 119
Dickson Street 98
Diering, Chuck 173
Doak, Bill 63, 73
Dodier Avenue 27
Donaldson, John 54
Drew, J.D. 188
Dr. Martin Luther King Boulevard
        49

E

Easton Road 51
Eighth Street 39, 73, 195
Eleventh Street 169
Elizabeth Avenue 73, 91, 93, 144

Euclid Avenue 177
Evans, Dwight 157

F

Fairgrounds Hotel 99
Fairgrounds Park 17, 45, 99, 100, 127
Farrell, Eddie 82
Feller, Bob 134
First Presbyterian Church 71
Flood, Curt 148, 154
Forest Park Avenue 84
Foster, Rube 69
Freese, David 163
Frisch, Frankie 82

G

Gaedel, Eddie 134, 140, 177
Garagiola, Joe 93, 144, 146
Gateway Arch 150, 195
Gateway Archers 191
Geyer Road 75
Gibson, Bob 148, 152, 155, 166
Gleason, Bill 40, 43
Gleason, Jack 40, 43
Grand Boulevard 17, 21, 27, 30,
    53, 117
Gravois Road 43, 115, 146
Grbic Restaurant 141
Green, Scarborough 163
Guidry, Ron 157

H

Hamilton Avenue 63

Hamilton Hotel 63
Hamilton, Milo 144
Hancock, Josh 180
Hancock Place Elementary School
    144
Handlan, Alexander 53
Handlan's Park 53
Harris Stowe State University 80,
    91, 121
Hawthorne Place 109
Hearn, Jim 138
Hedges, Robert 51
Heine Meine Field 107
Hemus, Solly 148
Henderson, Rickey 173
Hernandez, Keith 157
Herzog, Whitey 161
Hickory Street 189
Hollocher, Charlie 108
Holly Avenue 69
Hornsby, Rogers 80
Horstman, Oscar 63
Hotel Jefferson 80
Howard, Elston 119
Howard, Ryan 163
Huggins, Miller 85
Hynes, Pat 49

I

Interstate 64 170, 180

J

Jack Patrick's Bar and Grill 40
Jacobson, Bill "Baby Doll" 66
James "Cool Papa" Bell Avenue 98

Jefferson Avenue 37
Jefferson Barracks National
    Cemetery 141, 173
Jennings, Bill 140, 173
Joe Fassi Sausage and Sandwich
    Factory 104
Johnson, Walter 113
John Weber Drive 173
Jones, Sam "Toothpick" 90

K

Keane, Johnny 142, 148, 154
Keokuk Street 140
King, Charles "Silver" 41
King, Ray 188
Kingshighway Boulevard 103, 131
KMOX 7, 13, 61, 86, 146, 184

L

Lackland Avenue 8
Laclede Avenue 53, 89
Lafayette High School 163
Lafayette Park 19
LaRussa, Tony 132
LaSalle Street 65, 86
Lemay Ferry Road 106
Lemon, Bob 134
Leonard, Dutch 153
Lester's Sports Bar & Grill 179
Lindbergh Boulevard 108
Lindell Boulevard 55, 110
Lindell Towers 110
Lindenwood University 41, 175,
    187
Livingston Avenue 10

Locust Street 57
Looper, Braden 181
Lou Brock Sports Complex 175
Lucas and Hunt Road 97
Lucas Avenue 73
Lucas, Henry 37
Lucas, J.B.C., II 24, 37
Lumiere Place Hotel and Casino
    163
Lynch Street 135
Lyons, Jimmie 98

M

MacKenzie Road 144
Magnolia Avenue 41
Manchester Road 134, 157
Mancuso, Gus 71
Marchetti Towers 55
Maris, Roger 159
Market Street 78, 159
Marquis, Jason 188
Marrero, Eli 188
Martin, Pepper 95
Mason Road 186
Mays, Willie 90, 138
McGee, Willie 157
McGinnis, George "Jumbo" 37
McGwire, Mark 151
McKnight Road 104
McLaughlin, Dan 185
McManus, Marty 107
Meadows, Lee 63
Medwick, Joe 95, 107, 186
Meine, Henry 106
Midland Boulevard 8
Mike Shannon's Steaks and Seafood
    161, 180

Miller, Bob 128
Mills, Charles 68
Missouri Avenue 19
Mize, Johnny 104
Molina, Yadier 189
Mount St. Rose Hospital 142
Mount Zion Baptist Church 121
Mueller, Don 128
Musial, Stan 99, 125, 129, 146,
    166, 179, 182, 186, 194,
    195

N

National Geospatial-Intelligence
    Agency 39, 45
Natural Bridge Avenue 17, 28, 45,
    99, 127
New St. Marcus Cemetery 43
Northland Avenue 117

O

Oakland Avenue 131
Old Meeting House Presbyterian
    Church Cemetery 78
Olive Street 39, 184
O'Neil, Buck 174
One Memorial Way 185
Ozzie's Restaurant and Sports Bar
    162

P

Paige, Satchel 98
Palermo's 122

Park Avenue 19
Park Pacific Building 185
Parkway Central High School 167
Pena, Tony 157
Pennsylvania Building 40
Plank, Eddie 54
Poplar Street 169
Potomac Street 142
Prairie Avenue 46
Prescott Avenue 69
Prince, Bob 132
Pujols, Albert 163, 182
Pulaski Avenue 61

R

Rawlings, George and Alfred 73
Rawlings Sporting Goods 13, 73,
    158
Red Bird Bowling Lanes 146
Red Stockings Park 24
Reiser, Pete 128
Resurrection Cemetery 144
Reuss, Jerry 8, 108
Rickey, Branch 47, 67, 71, 78, 97,
    101
Ritenour High School 108
Robinson, Jackie 94
Robison Field 47, 53, 65, 101, 127
Robison, Frank and Stanley 47,
    55, 58
Ruth, Babe 13, 69, 76, 82, 84,
    105, 165

S

Saigh, Fred 136

Scherzer, Max 167
Schilling, Curt 95
Schoendienst, Albert "Red" 141, 186
Schrader Funeral Home 134
Security Building 59
Seneca Lane 7
Sewell, Luke 110
Shannon, Mike 159, 185
Shenandoah Avenue 65, 103
Sherdel, Willie 63
Sheridan Road 171
Shocker, Urban 34
Sievers, Roy 128
Sisler, Dave 78
Sisler, Dick 78
Sisler, George 75, 82, 186, 194
Sit & Sip Lounge 123
Smith, Ozzie 157
Southwest High School 140
Southworth, Billy 110
Spink, Alfred H. 39
Spink, Charles 32, 40
Spink, J.G. Taylor 32, 40
Sportsman's Park 19, 27, 30, 45,
    51, 53, 67, 99, 101, 110, 117,
    121, 127, 131, 138, 150
Spring Street 121
Spruce Street 27, 169, 195
Stadium Plaza 150
St. Alphonsus Liguori Church 24
Stan Musial and Biggie's 129
Stanton, Tom 128
Stars Park 71, 78, 89
St. Charles Rock Road 148
Stengal, Casey 151
Stephens, Vern 107
St. Joseph's Academy 110
St. Louis Science Center 131
St. Louis University 55, 80, 191

St. Louis Walk of Fame 165
St. Lucas Cemetery 97
St. Peter's Cemetery 99
Strawberry, Darryl 175
Street, Charles "Gabby" 86, 99,
    185
Sublette Avenue 102
Sullivan Avenue 121
Sumner High School 89, 139
Sunset Memorial Park 117
Suttles, George "Mule" 79, 98
Suzuki, Ichiro 78

T

Tebeau, Oliver "Patsy" 57
Templeton, Garry 161
Tenace, Gene 162
Tennyson Avenue 8
Tenth Street 39
The Sporting News 13, 32, 39
Thomas, Lee 128
Tobin, John 65, 107
Toussaint L'Ouverture Elementary
    School 121
Trent Road 127
Trinity Avenue 165
Trouppe, Quincy 89
Tucker Boulevard 80, 113
Twelfth Street 135
Twenty-Second Street 43
Twenty-Third Street 75

U

Union Association Park 38
Union Boulevard 63

V

Vandeventer Avenue 46, 103
Vashon High School 89, 121
Veeck, Bill 140, 177
Virginia Avenue 61
Voit, Luke 163
von der Ahe, Chris 27, 30, 34, 44, 46, 67

W

Wainwright, Adam 188
Wainwright Tomb 32
Walnut Street 196
Washington Avenue 40, 163
Washington University Medical School 177
Weaver, Earl 117, 128
Welch, Curt 28
Wells, Willie 79, 98
West Florissant Avenue 32, 34
Westin Hotel 170
Westminster Place 67, 152
West Pine Mall 169
Westport Plaza 163
West Port Plaza Drive 161, 182
Westway Road 127
Williams, Dick 128
Williams, Ken 66
Woods Mill Road 167
Woodson Road 7
Wrigley, Philip 115

Y

Young, Cy 58, 153

ABOUT THE AUTHOR

Brian Flaspohler is a lifelong St. Louis Cardinals fan who grew up in a small town in central Missouri. He retired from a real job as a manufacturing engineer and now spends his days researching and writing about baseball history. He still watches the Cardinals but has officially reached the age where it is more fun to read about past baseball exploits than to watch the current game. He is a longtime member of the Society for American Baseball Research and a contributor to both the Bio Project and the Games Project. He has also written about the 1880s St. Louis Browns for a book on Sportsman's Park. When not occupied with baseball, he spends his time running the byways and trails in and around the St. Louis area. As of this writing, he has run every single day for over nine years.

Visit us at
www.historypress.com